PTSD

POST TRAUMATIC STRESS DISORDER

DR. RICHARD K. THOMAS

DEDICATED

TO

All who serve our country
To preserve our freedoms
To defend our democracy
And
Who have re-entered
Or
Who will re-enter
Life and living in these
United States of America

With
Special thoughts to our son:

Sergeant Steven P. Thomas
561st Military Police Cp,
716th Military Police BN,
16th Military Police BDE,
101st Airborne Division

SPECIAL THANKS TO

Major Nelson Borden
United States Army (Ret)

Major Glenn Hayden
United States Air Force (Ret)

Colonel Teddy Bitner
United States Army (Ret)

Pastor Bill Sweitzer
Specialist Fourth Class, United States Army (Ret)

Dr. Jamie Mogler
First Baptist Church, Bedford, Iowa
Pastor/Counselor

Mr. and Mrs. Tony and Patricia M. Cihak
Active Military and ADAF Military Spouse

For

Their valuable insights and perspectives
That guided the completion of this workbook.

FORWARD

It was an honor to have been asked by Dr. Thomas to review, and to comment on, his work "Post Traumatic Stress Disorder (PTSD): A Self-Study on Re-Entry into Life and Living."

Although I personally have never experienced PTSD, I have, in my military career, and in civilian and everyday life, witnessed cases of depression, loneliness, boredom, and in some cases, physical sickness, brought on by traumatic changes in lifestyle and environment.

In my humble opinion, Dr. Thomas has touched on more then PTSD in his study. When one is faced with major changes in life, we can find ourselves with challenges never before experienced. This study is a comprehensive look at mental, physical, and emotional problems, and offers the means in which to face them.

Dr. Thomas has effectively used the Scriptures to open up channels of thought, prayer, and the communing with God. Those avenues of thought, prayer, and talking with God are also effective ways to "come to grips" with many other physical, mental and emotional situations in which we may find ourselves.

It is evident that Dr. Thomas has spent a vast amount of time researching God's Word, as well as many other resources, to arrive at this point in the publication of his work. This study is indeed a life-changing "Re-Entry into Life and Living" self-help experience.

Nelson Borden, Major, United States Army (Ret).

CONTENTS

PREFACE

I know Post Traumatic Stress Disorder can be experienced by anyone who has witnessed or has been involved in a shocking event. But more and more these days our men and women in the armed forces are experiencing PTSD. This self-study workbook is geared toward our men and women serving in all branches of the United States military. This material can be used for other life shattering events that lead to PTSD. But my burden is for our military. There are three reasons why I undertook this project. First, I served during the Viet Nam era. Second, my son serves in the United States Army and has served in Iraq. You see how PTSD became near and dear to my heart. Third, I am a counselor who frequently counsels those suffering from PTSD, from survivors of September 11, people victimized by violence, and returning vets from hostile foreign soil.

Although this manual is geared toward our military personnel, an individual will find this material useful whatever the cause that generated PTSD. It is designed so that someone experiencing PTSD can complete each lesson and find comfort and practical biblical solutions in order to re-enter the normal mainstream of life and living.

The returning veteran with his /her spouse can use this self-study workbook. Both mates have undergone serious mental, emotional, and spiritual adjustments while the veteran was deployed. Both spouses were forced to make considerable adjustments during the deployment. Both mates carried a heavy load respectfully. Both mates must desire to bring the spiritual equilibrium back into their marriage. Both can find daily answers from each lesson so both can re-enter the normal mainstream of life and living.

A counselor working with someone who has PTSD can use this self-study workbook. Each chapter can be used during a counseling session, guiding the person toward personal application, or the work book can be used for weekly homework assignments to supplement the counseling session. The person the counselor is trying to help can benefit greatly from each lesson so he/she can re-enter the normal mainstream of life and living.

This self-study workbook could be used in a group counseling environment. However, the most beneficial way for someone to deal with PTSD and to re-enter the normal mainstream of life and living is individually with a counselor.

What this book will not do. This self-study workbook is not designed to present a classical analysis of PTSD. The Introduction will briefly provide scant basics of PTSD. Other authors have written on this topic with great skill. My intention is not to duplicate their efforts.

What this book can do. This self-study workbook is carefully and prayerfully written to provide biblical insights on major re-entry situations the veteran will face. Because I believe the Bible to be totally sufficient and Christ absolutely supreme, these studies are based on the Word of God.[1]

To understand life with all of its sadness and joy, one needs to know the Author of Life and the Creator of the Universe. One needs to hear and accept Christ's invitation,

> "Come to Me, all who are weary and heavy-laden, and I will give you rest. Take My yoke upon you and learn from Me, for I am gentle and humble in heart, and YOU WILL FIND REST FOR YOUR SOULS. For My yoke is easy and My burden is light" (Matthew. 11:28-30).

I am confident, if you will honesty search these Scriptures and apply the principles, your re-entry into life and living will be exceedingly more than you ever could think or image (Ephesians 3:20). Christ wants you to enjoy life, but to enjoy it more abundantly (John 10:10). Remember that as you draw near to God, God will draw near to you (James 4:8). God bless you.

A Postscript: The version of the Bible used in these lessons is the New American Standard Version (NASB).

---

1. All Scriptures are taken from the New American Standard Version of the Bible unless otherwise noted in the lesson.

What is Post Traumatic Stress Disorder?

Post-traumatic stress disorder (PTSD) develops after a terrifying ordeal that involved physical harm or the threat of physical harm. The person who develops PTSD may have been the one who was harmed, the harm may have happened to a loved one, or the person may have witnessed a harmful event that happened to loved ones or strangers.

PTSD was first brought to public attention in relation to war veterans, but it can result from a variety of traumatic incidents, such as mugging, rape, torture, being kidnapped or held captive, child abuse, car accidents, train wrecks, plane crashes, bombings, or natural disasters such as floods or earthquakes.[2]

Post-traumatic stress disorder symptoms can come and go. You may have more symptoms during times of higher stress or when you experience symbolic reminders of what you went through. For example, some people whose PTSD symptoms had been gone for years saw their symptoms come back again with the terrorist attacks in the U.S. on Sept. 11, 2001.[3]

Researchers are still trying to understand what causes someone to get post-traumatic stress disorder. Researchers don't know exactly what causes post-traumatic stress disorder.[4]

There are no tests to diagnose PTSD. Post-traumatic stress disorder is diagnosed based on signs, symptoms, and a thorough psychological evaluation. Your doctor or mental health professional will ask you to describe the signs and symptoms you're experiencing — what they are, when they occur, how intense they are and how long they last. Your doctor also might ask you to describe the event that led up to your symptoms. You may also have a physical exam to check for any other medical problems.[5]

Among American Vietnam theater veterans, 31% of the men and 27% of the women have had PTSD in their lifetime. Preliminary findings suggest that

---

2. www.NIMH.org (National Institute for Mental Health)
3. www.mayoclinic.org
4. IBID, Mayo Clinic
5. IBID, Mayo Clinic

PTSD will be present in at least 18% of those serving in Iraq and 11% of those serving in Afghanistan. PTSD has been observed in all veteran populations that have been studied, including World War II, Korean conflict, and Vietnam.[6] Post traumatic stress disorder is especially common among those who have served in combat, and it's sometimes called "shell shock," "battle fatigue" and "combat stress."[7]

Although most veterans do not develop PTSD, a sizeable minority will have PTSD for some period of their life. Preliminary findings suggest rates of PTSD will be at least 18% for Iraq veterans and 11% for Afghanistan veterans (2005). Those who served in the Persian Gulf, Operation Enduring Freedom, and Operation Iraqi Freedom experienced PTSD. It also has been found in United Nations peacekeeping forces deployed to other war zones around the world.

Frequent Combat Experiences Reported by Members of the U.S. Army, 2003 serving in Afghanistan and Iraq showed the following statistical information. The percentage for PTSD is highly probable for those serving in Iraq. A recent AP news article online discussed how Ft. Campbell, Kentucky has added fifty mental health professionals to help soldiers of the 101st Airborne Division to re-enter living in the United States because of the increase of PTSD as a leading cause of mental illness among soldiers. The chart below shows the percentages of military personnel encountering such life experiences from which PTSD could occur.

	Afghanistan	Iraq
Being attacked or ambushed	58%	89%
Receiving incoming fire	84%	86%
Being shot at	66%	93%
Seeing dead bodies or remains	39%	95%
Knowing someone seriously injured or killed	43%	86%

People with PTSD may startle easily, become emotionally numb (especially in relation to people with whom they used to be close), lose interest in things they used to enjoy, have trouble feeling affectionate, be irritable, become more

6. The National Center for Post Traumatic Stress Disorder; the United States Department of Veterans Affairs.

7. IBID; Mayo Clinic

aggressive, or even become violent. They avoid situations that remind them of the original incident, and anniversaries of the incident are often very difficult. PTSD symptoms seem to be worse if the event that triggered them was deliberately initiated by another person, as in a mugging or a kidnapping. Most people with PTSD repeatedly relive the trauma in their thoughts during the day and in nightmares when they sleep. These are called flashbacks. Flashbacks may consist of images, sounds, smells, or feelings, and are often triggered by ordinary occurrences, such as a door slamming or a car backfiring on the street. A person having a flashback may lose touch with reality and believe that the traumatic incident is happening all over again.[8]

Not every traumatized person develops full-blown or even minor PTSD. Symptoms usually begin within 3 months of the incident but occasionally emerge years afterward. They must last more than a month to be considered PTSD. The course of the illness varies. Some people recover within 6 months, while others have symptoms that last much longer. In some people, the condition becomes chronic.[9]

We know that you have seen things that escape the comprehension of the human mind. We know that you have done things that the human mind could never grasp or fathom. We know you have lived in dreadful conditions, endure environmentally harsh elements, suffered great physical adjustments, but you are now home. Welcome home soldier. We (America) owe you a debt of gratitude. Words seem woefully shallow in expressing our deepest appreciation for what you have and are doing. I, a fellow United States Army sergeant, offer this book with the deepest hope that it can help you re-enter life and live to the fullest.

8. IBID; NIMH
9. IBID; NIMH

LESSON 1

Do You Have Peace with God?

Therefore, having been justified by faith,
we have peace with God
through our Lord Jesus Christ (Romans 5:1)

Write a paragraph on what you think it means to have peace with God.

Many people believe they can have peace with God by working for it. Read Romans 4:1-4 and answer the following questions.

1. *Was Abraham justified (justify means God declares someone in right standing with Him) by something he did?*

2. *According to verse 3, if Abraham were justified before God by doing something, how would Abraham have responded?*

3. According to verse 4, if someone works for something, what do they expect?

4. According to verses 3 and 5, how was Abraham justified?

Many people believe they can have peace with God by keeping a set of rules like the Ten Commandments. Read Romans 4:13-15 and answer the following questions.

1. According to verse 13, Abraham was not made heir of the world by....?

2. If someone could keep the Law, what two things take place?

3. According to verse 15, what does the Law bring about?

Read Galatians 3:2. How did the Galatian saints receive the Spirit?

Read 1 Peter 1:5-16. What does God command?

Read James 2:10. Can someone keep the whole law? If not, what does the Bible say about the person who does not keep the whole law?

Define the concept of sin in a few sentences.

Jesus said sin is both an action and attitude. Sin is not restricted to what someone else sees, but includes what God sees. That is why Jesus said sin is both an action and attitude. The act of sin is the outworking of a sinful attitude. You cannot murder someone if you do not hate him or her in your heart. Write down the action and attitude of sin from the following verses.

Matthew 5:21: Action is _____ *Attitude is* _____

Matthew 5:27: Action is _____ *Attitude is* _____

Matthew 5:38: Action is _____ *Attitude is* _____

Matthew 5:43: Action is _____ *Attitude is* _____

According to Romans 5:12, how did sin come into the world?

Has everyone sinned? (Romans 3:23)

What is the penalty for sin? (Romans 6:23)

What do the following verses say about getting rid of my sin and being saved?

- *Acts 2:37-38*

- *Romans 10:9-10*

- *Mark 16:16*

- *John 3:16-18*

- *John 10:9*

- *Acts 4:12*

- *Acts 16:31*

- *Ephesians 2:8-9*

- *Titus 3:5*

Once a person accepts Christ as their Savior and Lord, what do the following verses say about that decision?

- *1 Peter 1:3-5*

- *Romans 8:1-2*

What has God the Father, God the Son, and God the Holy Spirit done for you according to Ephesians 1:3-14?

God the Father has [1] _____ & [2] _____

God the Son has [1] _____ & [2] _____

God the Spirit has [1] _____ & [2] _____

According to 1 John 5:13, what assurance can you have if you made the decision to believe on and follow Christ?

According to John 10:10, what kind of life is Christ offering to you?

What do you think that would look like?

According to John 10:28, what is Christ giving to the person who truly believes?

What will never happen to the person who truly believes?

According to 2 Corinthians 5:17, what has happened to you?

_____

Friend, have you made such a commitment? Are you a child of God by faith in the work of Jesus Christ at Calvary? Can you remember a time when you invited Christ into your life to cleanse you from your sin and receive you as His child? If not, you can do it right now by praying this prayer with a truly humble and repentant heart.

Lord Jesus, I am now aware of my sin, and that my sin is an abomination to You. I know I am culpable for my sin and I truly deserve to live apart from You for all eternity. But You said in Your Word that if any man will confess with his mouth that Jesus is Lord and believe in their heart that God raised Jesus from the dead, I can be saved. Lord I believe. I confess my sin. I ask for Your forgiveness. Cleanse me of my sin. Accept me as your Child. I desire to live for You. I desire to know more and learn to enjoy the abundant life you have provided for me. Amen.

LESSON 2

Is God Really In Control?

God...He, who is the blessed and only Sovereign,
the King of kings and Lord of lords (1 Timothy 6:15)

Someone has penned these words to describe the sovereignty of God. "God in His love always wills what is best for us. In His wisdom, He always knows what is best, and in His sovereignty He has the power to bring it about."

Someone who is experiencing a life shattering event may wonder if God is really in control. Rabbi Harold S. Kushner wrote a national best selling book entitled, *When Bad Things Happen to Good People*. Rabbi Kushner concludes that the author of the book of Job "is forced to choose between a good God who is not totally powerful, or a powerful God who is not totally good. God wants the righteous to live peaceful, happy lives, but sometimes even He can't bring that about." When faced with such horrific violent acts, many people struggle with God being all-powerful but allows such ghastly acts.

Did you ever feel this way when you were deployed? Did you experience these feelings after the damaging events you experienced? Do you ever feel this way since being stateside? Can God really be both good and powerful and be in control? Is God good? Is God all powerful?

Set aside some time to slowly, methodically, and thoughtfully look up each of these Scriptures and write down what they have to say about God's sovereignty.

- *2 Kings 19:15*

- *Job 26:13*

- *Job 38:4*

- *Job 23:13*

- *Pr. 3:19*

- *Isaiah 42:5*

- *Isaiah 44:6*

- *Isaiah 45:12*

- *Isaiah 66:2*

- *Job 2:10*

- *Job 12:13-14*

- *Proverbs 16:4*

- *Amos 3:6*

- *Jonah 1:9*

- *Revelation 1:8*

- *Revelation 3:14*

- *Revelation 4:11*

- *Hebrews 11:3*

- *Romans 11:35-36*

- *Habakkuk 1:1-11*

- *Isaiah 10:5-6*

- *Isaiah 10:7-11*

- *Isaiah 10:12-16*

- *Genesis 14:19, 22*

- *Psalm 24:1*

- *Isaiah 54:5*

- *Daniel 4:17, 25*

- *Job 5:10*

- *Matthew 5:45*

- *Psalm 104:4*

- *Psalm 65:9*

- *Hosea 2:8*

Write a summary of the truths you learned about the sovereignty of God. Be specific. Take your time.

1._____

2._____

3._____

4._____

5._____

6._____

7._____

8._____

9._____

10._____

Now, take some of these verses and write how you would apply it to the trauma you witnessed. What verses would specifically help you right now in accepting God's control and your responsibility to those events? Remember, "God in His love always wills what is best for you. In His wisdom, He always knows what is best, and in His sovereignty He has the power to bring it about."

LESSON 3

Dealing with My Past

I do not regard myself as having laid hold of it yet; but one thing I do:
forgetting *what lies behind and reaching forward to what lies ahead,*
I press on toward the goal
for the prize of the upward call of God in Christ Jesus
(Philippians 3:13-14)

Everyone has an irrevocable past. What is done is done. It can never be changed or recalled. Lord Byron, the English poet, once wrote, "No hand can make the clock strike for me the hours that are past."

One can only imagine the horrific things that you might have experienced. Death, disease, search and destroy mission, insurgent detail, and much more. No one can fully comprehend military life, especially if you are a believer in the Lord Jesus Christ and you serve those who are far from God as their Creator let alone Savior. You may have been given orders, commands, or situations that require instant obedience with no pre-thought as to the results or consequences.

The person who penned Philippians had a terrible past. Read Acts 9:1-2, 14 and 21. Record what type of person Paul was, and what he did.

Read Acts 22:4-5. Record how Paul described himself and what he intended to do.

Read Acts 26:9-11. Record how Paul describes himself and what he intended to do.

Look up Acts 9:3-16. What happened to Paul?

Read Acts 22:6-14. What happened to Paul?

Read Acts 26:12-18. What happened to Paul?

Even though Paul was forgiven, and God would use Paul greatly, how did Paul view himself? (1 Corinthians 15:9; Ephesians 3:8; 1 Timothy 1:15).

Read Philippians 3:12-14 at least five times. After reading this passage five times, answer the following questions.

A. *What is Paul referring to when he writes, "not that I have already obtained or have already become perfect"?*

B. What do you think Paul means when he says, "I press on"?

C. What do you think Paul is referring to when he writes, "That I may lay hold of that for which also I was laid hold of by Christ Jesus"?

D. What is the significance of "but one thing I do"?

4. Make a list of everything Paul refers to when he says, "forgetting what lies behind." Think through Paul's life and list the positive and negative things Paul included in this phrase.

5. What are some things that Paul would be "reaching forward to what lies ahead?"

6. What image comes to mind when Paul writes, "I press on toward the goal?" Remember, Paul liked to use metaphors about athletes.

Three verbs (action words) that Paul uses would summarize these verses. What are they?

F_____ the past

R_____ forward

P_____ on toward

——————————————

Do you believe that if God was able to forgive and use Paul, that God can do the same for you? If not, make a list of those things you've done that you think God can't forgive.

Read the following verses and write down what they say about God's forgiveness.

- *Psalm 25:18*

- *Psalm 65:3*

- *Psalm 79:9*

- *Psalm 86:5*

- *Psalm 103:12*

- *Psalm 145:8*

- *Isaiah 43:25*

- *Jeremiah 3:12*

- *Joel 2:13*

Hebrews eleven is called the Hall of Faith. In this chapter, the writer of Hebrews lists men and women who demonstrated great faith. But they are just that, men and women. No super heroes, no credentials, and frankly, nothing to write home about. Read Hebrews 11. Then list each person's struggles he or she experienced in life. You may need to read about their lives from the Old Testament for a greater grasp of what their lives were like. Reflect on what you can learn from them and record your insights under "Lessons for me" section of this chart. This exercise is to help you see that regardless of what I have done in the past God wants to use me.

Character	Struggle	Lesson for me
Abel		
Enoch		
Abraham		
Sarah		
Isaac		
Jacob		
Joseph		

Moses		
Rahab		
Gideon		
Barak		
Samson		
Jephthah		
David		
Samuel		

Take this space to record additional insights you learned.

Often we assume that God is unable to work in spite of
our weaknesses, mistakes, and sins.
We forget that God is a specialist; he is well able to work
our failures into his plans.
Erwin W. Lutzer (1941–)

LESSON 4

I Feel Guilty

Psychiatrists require many sessions to relieve a patient of guilt feelings which have made him sick in body and mind, Jesus' power of spiritual and moral persuasion was so overwhelming that he could produce the same effect just by saying: Thy sins are forgiven thee.
Malcolm Muggeridge (1903–1990)

Using a good dictionary, write out at least three different definitions for guilt.

Now, develop and write out your own definition of guilt.

Read the following verses and write down what makes people feel guilty.

- *Genesis 3:1-13*

- *Genesis 4:1-10*

- *Genesis 42:21*

- *Numbers 5:6*

- *Ezra 10:10*

- *Job 10:7*

- *Psalm 32:1-5*

- *1 Corinthians 11:27*

- *James 2:10*

A biblical definition of guilt is "a legal or judicial term that implies criminal responsibility in the eyes of a court of law, whether human or divine."

Three Greek word groupings provide helpful insight on the concept of guilt.

Aita means the grounds, cause, reason, charge, or motive for guilt. Record how the following verses illustrate the meaning of this word.

- *Matthew 19:3*

- *Matthew 27:37*

Eleychoo means to bring to light, expose, set forth, convict, convince, and provide evidence for the charge. Record how the following verses illustrate the meaning of this word.

- *1 Timothy 5:20*

- *2 Timothy 4:2*

- *Titus 2:15*

Enochos means a liability, deserving of a penalty in keeping with the charge (aitia) and evidence (eleychoo). Record how the following verses illustrate the meaning of this word.

- *Matthew 5:21*

- *James 2:10*

> Guilt is exposing someone's actions, identifying the reasons for those actions, and assessing an appropriate punishment to restore the offender to God and his fellow man.

Read Genesis 3:7-13. How did Adam and Eve handle their guilt?

Adam and Eve _____ up the problem

Adam and Eve _____ from God

Adam and Eve _____ avoided the real issue

Adam and Eve _____ blamed others for the problem

People can produce guilt in the lives of others through manipulative tactics in order to control the person. Are you experiencing this? If so, please record what is happening, who is involved, and what do you think is motivating that person(s) to respond to you as they do?

Read Galatians 6:1. God uses people to produce guilt in the lives of others using the Word of God with the sole purpose of restoration. Do you have guilt because someone is lovingly sharing God's Word with you about an attitude or action you are displaying that is harmful to yourself and others? Please describe.

Biblically and ultimately, the Holy Spirit convicts of sin and the human mind interacts with this convicting work to produce guilt

Read Job 10:14 and Psalm 32:5. Guilt is a direct result of sinful actions. Can you list any?

Read Hosea 5:15. Guilt must be acknowledged before God grants forgiveness. Can you remember doing this? Are you willing to acknowledge your sin before God right now?

Read Hosea 10:2. A person bears unnecessary guilt because of lack of faith. Do you believe God will forgive you? If not, what did you do that is so terrible God wouldn't forgive you?

Read 1 John 1:9 and Psalm 32:5. Forgiveness is available for all sin and the associated guilt. If you confessed your sin, list your feelings of guilt. Then, "Thank God" for cleansing you of those feelings also.

Read Leviticus chapters 5-6. In the Old Testament, what sacrifice could a person with a guilty conscience offer to God?

Read Isaiah 53:10. Who replaced the Old Testament guilt offering?

Read John 1:29. Jesus is called the Lamb of God. According to this verse, what did He alone do?

Read Job 33:9. A counselee can live guilt free. Do you believe that you can live free from guilt?

Read the following verses and record what God will do for you.

- *Isaiah 25:8*

- *Ezekiel 36:26*

- *Zechariah 3:4*

Read the following verses and record what God will do for you.

- *Psalm 6:2*

- *Psalm 41:1*

- *Jeremiah 17:14*

- *Jeremiah 30:17*

Read the following verses, and write down what God will do with your sin and guilt.

- *Psalm 103:2-5*

- *Revelation 1:5*

- *Psalm 103:10*

- *Isaiah 1:18*

- *Isaiah 38:17*

- *Isaiah 43:25*

- *Isaiah 44:22*

On the following page, write a prayer of thanksgiving and praise for God's desire and willingness to cleanse you from any guilt and sin. Write it out as if you were talking to Him. Be thoughtful and appreciative.

Dear God...

The purpose of being guilty is to bring us to Jesus. Once we are there, then its purpose is finished. If we continue to make ourselves guilty—to blame ourselves—then that is sin in itself. Corrie ten Boom (1892–1983)

LESSON 5

What Do I Do With This Sense of Shame?

Fear not, for you will not be put to shame;
And do not feel humiliated, for you will not be disgraced **(Isaiah. 54:4a)**

By definition, shame is the feeling someone experiences because of another who has mistreated him or her and the conflict remains unresolved.

Read the following verses and write down what they have to say about shame.

- *Numbers 12:14*

- *2 Samuel 19:5*

- *Psalm 69:19*

- *2 Thessalonians 3:14*

- *Hebrews 12:2*

There is one Greek word for shame (<u>aischune</u>). This word means dishonor or disfigured. Someone who experiences shame feels dishonored, or they feel like others think something is wrong with them.

Read Genesis 37-50. In what ways did Joseph experience shame?

Read Daniel 1. In what ways did Daniel have a sense of shame?

Read Hebrews 12:1-3 and 1 Peter 2:22-24. In what ways did Jesus face shame?

Did Joseph, Daniel, or Jesus do anything wrong to endure this sense of shame?

Is shame a result of someone sinning or the result of being sinned against by another? Explain your answer.

All three biblical personalities have a common thread.

1. *All understood and accepted the sovereign plan and purposes of God. How do you see this?*

2. *All fulfilled their personal responsibilities. Document how they fulfilled their responsibilities.*

3. *All avoided the personal justification to develop a life of sin in response to their particular situation. Record how you see this.*

Read the following verses and write how each verse gives hope for a person experiencing shame.

- *1 Corinthians 10:13*

- *Ephesians 3:20*

- *Hebrews 6:19-20*

- *Psalm 145:5-6*

- *1 Peter 1:3*

- *Ephesians 1:3*

- *2 Corinthians 9:8*

- *Lamentations 3:32*

- *Psalm 42:5, 11*

- *Psalm 43:1*

- *1 Thessalonians 1:3*

- *2 Peter 1:3*

How has this lesson helped you deal with your sense of shame?

LESSON 6

Memories and Flash Backs

We are destroying speculations and every lofty thing raised up against the knowledge of God, and we are taking every thought captive to the obedience of Christ (2 Corinthians 10:5)

Flashbacks are memories of past traumas. They may take the form of pictures, sounds, smells, body sensations, feelings, or the lack of them (numbness). Many times, there is no actual visual or auditory memory. One may have the sense of panic, being trapped, feeling powerless with no memory stimulating it. These experiences can also happen in dreams.

Flashbacks or memories are directly related to your mind and thought processes. This Bible study will show you how to control your thought life. You will learn how to deal with the flashbacks as you re-enter life and living.

What is the thought life? It is the God-given ability to process sensory and non-sensory data whereby you reach a conclusion and then act in accordance with that conclusion. A person's thought life will influence their emotional life and to-gether (thought life + emotions) will control each subsequent choice. Amy Baker, a biblical counselor, coined the following phrase, "You do what you do, and you feel what you feel because of the way you think." Memorize this saying. It will be immensely helpful to you.

Look up each of the following verses and record what they have to say about a person controlling their thought life.

- *Proverbs 23:7a*

- *Romans 14:14*

- *James 1:26*

Look up the following verses and record how they illustrate what happens to a person who does or does not control their thoughts.

- *Genesis 26:7*

- *Nehemiah 6:9*

- *Philippians 1:17*

The condition of the mind produces corresponding actions.

The Bible describes what positive thinking should look like. Read the following Scriptures and write down how positive (good, righteous) thinking is described.

- *1 Chronicles 28:9*

- *Job 38:36*

- *Psalm 16:7*

- *Proverbs 18:15*

- *Isaiah 26:3*

- *Philippians 2:3*

- *2 Peter 3:1*

The Bible also describes negative thinking (ungodly, unrighteous). Read the following Scriptures and write down how negative thinking is described.

- *Exodus 10:10*

- *Nehemiah 6:8*

- *Job 15:35*

- *Proverbs 12:8*

- *Proverbs 17:20*

- *Romans 1:28*

- *1 Timothy 6:5*

- *2 Timothy 3:8*

- *Ephesians 4:17*

- *Colossians 1:21*

- *Colossians 2:18*

A believer lives in two worlds: God's and his own. Though redeemed and in the sanctification process (*doing wrong less and doing right more*), man's mind wrestles between good and evil, right and wrong, to obey or to disobey. For example, someone cuts you off on the freeway. You have a choice to go right (control your anger, not cuss or retaliate) or to do wrong (chase the car down, use sign language, cut back in front of that car and jam your brakes). What man thinks about will determine his behavior and relationship to God and others.

Read Romans 8:5-6. List the contrast in these verses.

Make a list of people, places, or things that stimulate your thinking in a good way.

Now make a list of people, places, and things that stimulate your thinking in a bad way.

Read the following verses and write out what the results are that a person can experience if he/she does not control their thoughts.

- *Philippians 4:7*

- *2 Corinthians 11:3*

- *1 John 5:21*

- *2 Peter 3:17*

> The fundamental exercise of any Christian, that every Christian can and must do, is to prepare his or her mind.

The following Scriptures teach that a person can control their thoughts. Read each verse and write out what it says about controlling your thoughts.

- *Ephesians 5:18*

- *Daniel 1:8*

- *Colossians 3:2*

Read these verses and record what Solomon is thinking. Record what conclusion Solomon reaches after thinking about those things.

- *Ecclesiastes 1:3*

- *Ecclesiastes 7:25*

- *Ecclesiastes 8:9*

What does Isaiah 43:18 say in reference to a person's thought life?

What does Paul says in Philippians 3:13 about your thinking?

According to Philippians 4:8, what are things we should think? List them.

Now define each of these words so you can understand them better.

Finally, write out one way you can begin to use each of these words to help you control your thought life. Take your time with this question. Be specific.

What does the Psalmist ask God to do for him in Psalm 26:2?

What does Jeremiah ask God to do in Jeremiah 17:10?

Study 2 Corinthians 10:4-5. Spend time carefully understanding the key words. Consult some good commentaries. After doing so, write out what you think the verse is saying and specifically how this verse can help you control your thought life.

As nothing is more easy than to think, so nothing is more difficult than to think well. Thomas Traherne (C. 1637–1674)

LESSON 7

What Do I Do When I Feel Fearful?

When I am afraid, I will put my trust in You (Psalm 56:3)

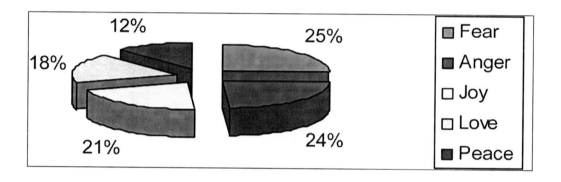

The chart above reveals three important facts.

1. *The emotion of fear ranks among the top five human responses to life.*

2. *The Bible deals more with fear than joy.*

3. *Fear separates the divine trio of love, joy, and peace, the core manifestation of the Fruit of the Spirit.*

The word <u>fear</u> is recorded 309 times in the Bible while the word <u>afraid</u> is recorded 164 times in the Bible. Often the source of our fear is the fear of man. The fear of man means I am more concerned with what others think, believe, or say about me than anything or anyone else. Another person who wants to harm you such as a military enemy, car-jacker, or thief can also generate the fear of man. This type of person often rearranges his/her life in order please others or to earn affection from someone.

Define fear, as you understand it.

Make a list of things you fear.

According to Proverbs 29:25, what is the result of fear?

According to Deuteronomy 6:13, what, or who should I fear.

Three other stages take place first before someone is dominated by fear. See diagram below.

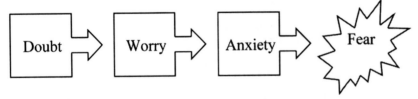

Doubt begins when someone initially questions God. Does God love me? Does God care what is happening in my life? Will God help me? Will God take care of me? Have you ever thought or expressed similar words? If so, when? To whom? About what?

If doubt is not controlled it paves the way for worry. Worry is the preoccupation of mind. It is what you think about the most. It is what your mind turns to when you am relaxed. If worry is not controlled, you will begin to have unexplained physical symptoms. Backaches, neck aches, headaches, shoulder, leg, hip pain. This will then lead to fear which is a complete domination and control of my life because of the way you are thinking. Do you experience this? What occupies your mind most? How much time do you spend thinking about "it?"

Fear is forgetful. It forgets what the Bible says about God in the midst of our fear. We need to remind ourselves of these truths for it is in knowing and believing these truths that we live in freedom (John 8:32).

Read the following verses and complete the sentence.

Numbers 14:9; 2 Chronicles 20:17; 32:7

God is _____ you.

Genesis 26:24; Deuteronomy 1:21

God_____ for you.

Haggai 2:5

God _____ His Word to you.

Nehemiah 4:14; Joel 2:21

God is _____ to you.

Deuteronomy 2:25

God goes _____ you and _____ your future.

Exodus 14:13; Isaiah 41:10

God _____ for you.

2 Kings 6

God's _____ are available to you.

Chronicles 28:20

God fulfills His _____ through you.

Isaiah 43:1; Matthew 10:11; Luke 12:7

God _____ you.

Genesis 21:17; Ruth 3:1

God _____ your prayers.

Joshua 1:8-9

God does not _____ your _____ against you.

Genesis 15:1; Psalm 27:1

God _____ you.

> Fear imprisons, faith liberates; fear paralyzes, faith empowers; fear
> disheartens, faith encourages; fear sickens, faith heals; fear makes
> useless, faith makes serviceable—and, most of all, fear puts hopelessness
> at the heart of life, while faith rejoices in its God.
> Harry Emerson Fosdick (1878–1969)

Answer the following questions the next time you are fearful.

1. What is happening when I feel fearful?

2. Who is directly or indirectly involved when I was feeling fearful?

3. What was I feeling at the time?

4. What was I thinking at the time I was fearful?

5. What did I want to happen to change the situation?

6. Did the situation change?

7. How did I feel if the situation changed?

8. How did I feel if the situation did not change?

Study the following Bible verses and list down some of the causes of fear.

- *Proverbs 28:1*

- *Proverbs 1:33*

- *Proverbs 29:25*

- *Psalm 23:4*

- *Psalm 56:4*

- *Psalm 46:2-3*

Have you experienced any of these causes? If so, please describe the circumstances.

Study the following Bible verses and write down some of the results of fear.

- *Proverbs 29:25*

- *Proverbs 10:24*

- *Proverbs 28:1*

- *Genesis 21:16-17*

- *Numbers 14:1-4*

Have you experienced any of these results? If so, please describe the circumstances.

Study the following Bible verses and list some of the solutions for fear.

- *2 Timothy 1:7*

- *Proverbs 3:21-25*

- *Hebrews 13:5-6*

- *Proverbs 14:26-27*

- *Psalm 34:4*

- *Proverbs 22:4*

- *1 John 4:18*

Select five things you were fearful of in the past. Now looking at the solutions for fear, see how many of the solutions you can match to your fears from the past. This exercise will help you recognize the causes of fear much earlier by being aware of what triggers your fears. It will also help you avoid the results of fear by properly matching up the right Bible verses to help you overcome your fear.

Fear knocked at the door. Faith answered. No one was there. Author unknown

LESSON 8

I Feel So Angry

Let all bitterness, wrath, anger, clamor, and slander be put away from you, along with all malice. Be kind to one another, tender-hearted, forgiving each other, just as God in Christ also has forgiven you
(Ephesians 4:31-32)

Anger is a reaction to situations that are judged as unfair, unjust, undeserved, unreasonable, excessive, inequitable, unwarranted, or biased. Anger can be expressed or suppressed. Anger can be internalized or externalized. Anger can seethe or explode or both. Whether a person expresses or suppresses his or her anger, it is damaging. It damages relationships. It hurts the marital relationship. Children can't understand why mommy or daddy is upset. Those living with you when you are angry, oftentimes feel they have done something wrong to upset you. When in reality, you are struggling with an unresolved situation, event, or circumstance. Why did God allow this terrible situation? Why did I have to experience the tragic death of someone I love? Why does God allow war, terrorism, and people using people cruelly?

But the Bible has great hope to help you cultivate self-control as you re-enter life and living with those you love and those who love you.

Take the following Anger Inventory Test (AIT). It is not scientific, but it may lend some insights on your anger. The rating scale is 1-5: 5=never; 4=seldom; 3=occasionally; 2=frequently; and 1=always.

_____ I become angry when someone hurts me.

_____ I become angry when someone is frustrated with me.

_____ I become angry when I feel betrayed.

_____ I become angry when others fail to see my point of view.

_____ I become angry when I don't get my own way.

_____ I become angry when someone else is angry.

_____ I become angry when I see someone else hurt by another.

_____ I become angry when I feel my opinion, advice, or counsel was ignored.

_____ I become angry when I feel like my authority is being challenged.

Record your score_____ .

There are two basic word groupings for the concept of anger. The first word grouping is from the Greek word _thymos_. The Latin word is _fumos_, which means smoke, steam, or breath. The word carries the idea of the soul being shown by its feelings and emotions. It is the outburst of anger or the display of anger. It is the expression of what someone is feeling on the inside. It can be pictured as a volcano. A volcano is unpredictable. It erupts when the pressure inside cannot be contained.

The second word grouping is from the Greek word _orge_. The word means puffed up, swelled, excited, naturally impulsive, temper, or a person's nature. In the classical Greek writings, it refers to the nose or the trembling nostrils of a horse snorting. It can be pictured as the boiling pot on the stove. The water heats up and rolls along the side of the pan but never boils over. This person is angry but tries to suppress or control the outward display.

Read the following Scriptures and write down what they have to say about anger.

- _Genesis 27:45_

- _Genesis 30:2_

- _Genesis 39:19_

- *Esther 1:12*

- *Exodus 32:19*

- *Numbers 24:10*

- *Judges 14:198*

- *Deuteronomy 19:6*

- *1 Samuel 17:28*

- *Esther 1:1*

- *1 Samuel 20:30*

- *Esther 5:9*

- *2 Samuel 12:5*

- *Proverbs 12:16*

Read the following Scriptures and record additional characteristics of someone who is angry. The lines will give you a hint on how many additional characteristics you should find.

Genesis 49:5-7

1._____

2._____

3._____

Job 36:18

1._____

Proverbs 11:23

1._____

Proverbs 21:14

1._____

Proverbs 27:4

1._____

Read the following verses and write down what the source of your anger could be.

- *James 4:1-2*

- *Acts 15:36-39*

Below is a list of underlying attitudes that perpetual anger. Check off all that apply.

❑ Attitudes	❑ Exasperation
❑ Partial obedience	❑ Conviction
❑ Unforgiving spirit	❑ Deception
❑ Personal agendas	❑ Lying
❑ Laziness	❑ Pride of correction
❑ Jealousy	❑ Self-righteousness
❑ Root of bitterness	❑ Unbiblical standards
❑ Spiritual apathy	❑ Distrust

Now, for all the ones you checked off, provide a recent example in the space below.

Before learning, what the Bible says about the wrong and right ways to express your anger, consider the following axioms.

1. Anger is something you do, not something that comes over you. Do you agree or disagree. Why?

2. Anger is a learned behavior. I agree or disagree. Why?

3. Anger is a moral issue. Agree or disagree. Why?

4. Anger is basic selfishness and idolatry. I agree or disagree. Why?

The following statements are lies.

1. Anger is something inside me. Why is this statement a lie?

2. It's OK to be angry with God. Why is this statement a lie?

3. My big problem is I am angry with myself. Why is this statement a lie?

Read the following Bible verses and write down the wrong ways to express your anger.

- Ephesians 4:26-27

- Proverbs 17:14

- Proverbs 29:11

- Proverbs 29:20

- Matthew 5:21-22

- Ephesians 4:31

- Proverbs 26:L21

- Proverbs 15:1

- Colossians 3:8

- Romans 12:17

- Romans 12:19

- *1 Peter 3:9*

- *1 Corinthians 13:5*

Go back through the verses now, and place a check "✓" by the ones you are most prone to do and provide a recent example.

Now look at the following Bible verses and write down what they have to say is the right way to express your anger. You will notice that some of the verses are the same as "wrong way to express your anger." The reason is that Proverbs often provides the wrong way and right way in the same verse. It is a Hebrew way of writing in the form of contrasts.

- *Romans 12:19-21*

- *Ephesians 4:26*

- *Ephesians 4:29*

- *Matthew 5:43-44*

- *Proverbs 19:11*

- *Proverbs 15:1*

- *Proverbs 15:28*

- *Proverbs 16:32*

- *Proverbs 25:28*

- *Proverbs 14:29*

Take a few minutes and try matching one of the correct ways of expressing your anger to one of the wrong ways you have been expressing your anger.

Read Matthew 5:1-12, Galatians 5:22-23, and 2 Peter 1:5-8. Below, make a list of the various Christian characteristics from these passages. There are nine (9) from Matthew (key is the word blessed); there are nine (9) from Galatians, and there are 8 from 2 Peter. Then rate yourself on a scale of 1-5: 5=never; 4=seldom; 3=occasionally; 2=frequently; and 1=always.

Characteristic	Personal Evaluation

Reflect back on the last time you got angry and answer the following questions. Be truthful and honest. That is the only way you can begin to exercise self-control.

1. Did you get angry about the right thing?[10]

2. Did you express your anger the right way?

3. How long did your angry last?

4. How controlled was your anger?

5. What motivated your anger?

---

10 I am indebted to David Powlison for these question from his three-part article on Anger in the <u>Journal of Biblical</u> Counseling (Vol. 14, No. 1, 1995; Vol. 14, No. 2, 1996; Vol. 16. No. 1. 1997)

6. Is your anger "primed and ready" to respond to another's habitual sin?

7. What was the effect of your anger?

Here are eight questions you need to memorize. They will help you process the next angry situation so you can respond with self-control. Why not work through these questions using a previous situation in which you were angry?

1. What is the situation I am angry about?

2. How am I reacting?

3. What is my motivation? (What do I really want?)

4. What will be the consequences if I get angry?

5. What is true about this situation?

6. What specific things can I do to turn to God for help?

7. How should I respond in this situation to glorify God?

8. What will be the rewards of my faith and obedience to the biblical way to handle my anger?

Additional space for recording your insights.

Oftentimes anger is related to the "rights" issue. Complete the following Study Guide to help you understand if your anger is related to what you think is a right.

Check off which of the following you consider your "rights."

❑ Right to have and control personal belongings

❑ Right to privacy

❑ Right to have and express personal opinions

❑ Right to earn and use money

❑ Right to plan your own schedule

❑ Right to respect

❑ Right to have and choose friends

❑ Right to belong, be loved and be accepted

❑ Right to be understood

❑ Right to be supported

❑ Right to make your own decisions

❑ Right to determine your own future

❑ Right to have good health

❑ Right to date

❑ Right to be married

❑ Right to have children

❑ Right to be considered worthwhile and important

❑ Right to be protected and cared for

❑ Right to be appreciated

❑ Right to travel

❑ Right to have the job you want

❑ Right to a good education

❑ Right to be a beautiful person

❑ Right to be treated fairly

❑ Right to be desired

❑ Right to have fun

❑ Right to raise children your way

❑ Right to security and safety

❑ Right to fulfilled hopes and aspirations

❑ Right to be successful

❑ Right to have others obey you

❑ Right to have your own way

❑ Right to be free of difficulties and problems

Now, complete the following chart. Which of the above mentioned "rights" you checked off are you being denied, and by whom?

Right	By Whom

If you are a Christian, you and all that you have (your rights included) belong to God. Read the following verses and record what they say about your "rights."

1 Corinthians 6:19-20
Romans 12:1
Psalm 24:1
1 Corinthians 9:6-12
1 Corinthians 9:18
2 Thessalonians 3:9

Rights that cause fights are plights! - rkt

Go back and look at your "rights" and who is denying you those rights. In light of these Scriptures, rethink what it might look like if you chose to give up your rights instead of fighting for them.

Fighting for my "rights"	Giving up my "rights"
Right to make my own decisions	I will be a wise person if I seek additional advice from dad and mom. They are older, wiser and have probably experienced what I am going through. Only a foolish person refuses the counsel of his parents (Pr. 11:14; 15:22; 24:6; 10:8; 12:15; 14:16; 15:5)

Hot heads and cold hearts never solved anything. Billy Graham (1918–)

Use the following chart to begin to practice giving up your rights and trusting God. Each time you feel your "rights" are being violated, complete the following chart.

My "right"	Violated by whom?	How I will give up my "rights"

To reply to a nasty remark with another nasty remark is like
trying to remove dirt with mud.
Author unknown

You have a vast amount of information to handle your anger. Premeditation is preparation (Daniel 1:8). Think ahead. In the space below, write out your "Action Plan" for the next time you get angry. Think about what things you get angry about most frequently. For example, "When my wife spends more money for something than what we budgeted, instead of getting angry, I will…"

LESSON 9

Why Do I Worry or Feel Anxious?

*Do not worry then, saying, 'What will we eat?' or 'What will we drink?'
or 'What will we wear for clothing?' For the Gentiles eagerly seek all
these things; for your heavenly Father knows that you need all
these things. But seek first His kingdom and His righteousness,
and all these things will be added to you. So do not worry
about tomorrow; for tomorrow will care for itself.
Each day has enough trouble of its own*
(Matthew 6:31-34)

What is worry? In the Bible, worry is to be overly concerned about something. The root word for worry comes from the word anxious or anxiety. Worry or anxiety is usually about something pertaining to the next day; tomorrow. Someone has rightly said, "Worry is the interest we pay on tomorrow's troubles." Sarah Orne Jewett (1849–1909) said, "Tain't worthwhile to wear a day all out before it comes."

People worry about their jobs. Will they still have one? With lay-offs and recession, will my company downsize? When they become preoccupied with that thought, they begin to think about how to pay the mortgage? Will the bank foreclose on their home? What about the necessities like food, clothing, and cable? Will my wife have to return to work? What about our children's college tuition payments? If I don't have a job, then I won't have health insurance. What if I wind up in the hospital? Without a job, I can't afford life insurance! What if I die? How will my wife and kids manage?

Make a list in the space below about the things you worry about.

Read Matthew 6:25-34 and answer the following questions.

1. Jesus defines "life" as what three basic things?

2. Do you have need of these basic things?

3. What is Jesus' first illustration?

4. Birds cannot do three things. List them.

5. How does Jesus describe God in relation to the birds?

6. What does their Heavenly Father do for them?

7. Jesus concludes verse 26 with what question?

8. What makes this question important to you?

9. What does verse 27 mean to you and your situation?

10. What is the second illustration that Jesus uses in verse 28?

11. Explain verses 28-30

12. What makes this question important to you?

13. Whom does Jesus refer to who worries?

14. According to verse 32, is God aware of our needs?

15. Instead of focusing on what we will eat, drink and wear, what should you be concentrating on according to verse 33

16. How would you do this?

17. What is Christ's warning in verse 34?

A widow who had successfully raised a very large family was being interviewed by a reporter. In addition to six children of her own, she had adopted 12 other youngsters, and through it all, she had maintained stability and an air of confidence. When asked the secret of her outstanding accomplishment, her answer to the newsman was quite surprising. She said, "I managed so well because I'm in a partnership!" "What do you mean?" he inquired. The woman replied, "Many years ago I said, 'Lord, I'll do the work and You do the worrying.' And I haven't had an anxious care since." We could all profit by following the example of that mother. When we carry our part of the load, we need not be disturbed by the demands of life.

Read Psalm 94:19 and answer the following questions

1. How do anxious thoughts multiply in a person?

2. What does the word <u>consolation</u> mean? You might need to look up the word in a dictionary.

3. How do consolations delight one's soul?

Read Psalm 139:23-24 and answer the following questions.

1. What does the Psalmist want God to do?

2. Can anxiety be harmful to a person? If so, how?

3. What does the Psalmist ask God to do in verse 24?

Read Isaiah 35:4. Judah is surrounded by enemies. God is commanding the prophet Isaiah to address Judah's anxiety. There are four words of encouragement God wants Isaiah to speak. Complete the chart below.

The Word of encouragement to Judah	Why do you think Judah would need this?	How can you use this in your situation
Take courage		
Fear not		
God will come		
He will save you		

Read Jeremiah 17:8 and explain how this verse will help you deal with your anxiety?

Read Philippians 4:4-8 and answer the following questions.

1. According to verse 4, what am I to do when I am anxious?

2. How often am I to do this?

3. What is a gentle spirit? How does anxiety disrupt a gentle spirit?

4. What message do I communicate when I am anxious?

5. Verse 6 begins with a command. What is it?

6. Verse 6 lists four things I should do when I am anxious. What are they?

7. What is the result of obeying verse 6 according to verse 7?

8. List what I am to think about instead of the problem?

Write out what you have learned and what action steps you will take when you worry or are anxious in the space below.

According to the National Bureau of Standards, a dense fog covering seven city blocks to a depth of 100 feet is composed of something less than one glass of water. That is, all the fog covering seven city blocks 100 feet deep could be, if it were gotten all together, held in a single drinking glass; it would not quite fill it. This can be compared to the things we worry about. If we could see into the future and if we could see our problems in their true light, they wouldn't blind us to the world – to living itself – but instead could be relegated to their true size and place. And if all the things most people worry about were reduced to their true size, you could probably stick them all into a water glass, too.

LESSON 10

Depression

> *If depression is creeping up and must be faced,*
> *learn something about the nature of the beast:*
> *You may escape without a mauling.*
> *Dr. R. W. Shepherd*

Depression is a debilitating mood, feeling, or attitude of hopelessness. A person can feel overwhelmed with life. Depression can hide behind a pleasant smile and laughter, but inside you may feel lonely, isolated, and think that nobody really cares; and if they did, they would not know how to help you because they are not going through what you have gone through.

Depression can affect a person's physical well being. Unexplained aches and pains are often apart of depression. Does this describe you? If so, make a list of physical problems you are experiencing.

Depression can affect a person's emotional stability. Mood swings, irritability, and weepiness are easily triggered. Does this describe you? If so, describe your moods when you feel depressed.

Depression can affect a person's mental steadiness. Some complain that they cannot shut their mind off. They say their thoughts are constantly racing. It disturbs their sleep. Does this describe you? If so, make a list of all the things that occupy your thought life.

Read Genesis 4:1-11 and answer the following questions.

1. What is the relationship between Cain and Abel?

2. What were the occupations of Cain and Abel?

3. What kind of offering did Cain being to the Lord?

4. What kind of offering did Abel bring to the Lord?

5. Whose offering did the Lord accept?

6. What was Cain's reaction?

7. What did God point out to Cain in verse 6?

8. What did God instruct Cain to do in verse 7?

9. What does anger want to do according to verse 7?

10. What is the relationship between anger and depression?

11. Did Cain tell his brother what God said?

12. Did Cain accept God's counsel?

13. *What did Cain do?*

14. *How did God punish Cain?*

15. *What do you think was at the heart of Cain's depression?*

16. *Record what you learned from this passage before going to the next passage.*

Read First Samuel chapters 18-31 and answer the following questions.

1. *Who is Saul?*

2. *What caused Saul to turn against David?*

3. Record the various words/actions the Bible uses to describe Saul's emotions toward David. Read 1 Samuel 18:8, 9, 11, 12, 13, 15, 17, 21, and 28.

4. What are the various relationships Saul uses to try and capture David?

5. What drove Saul to try and destroy David?

6. How many times was Saul's life spared by David? Each time, how did Saul describe David and describe himself? (1 Samuel chapters 24 and 26)

7. How did Saul's life end?

8. What do you think was at the heart of Saul's depression? (See also 1 Samuel 13 and 15)

9. Record what you learned from this passage before going to the next passage.

Read 2 Samuel 11-12, Psalm 32 and Psalm 51 and answer the following questions.

1. According to 1 Sam. 11:1, where should David have been?

2. Why do you think David could not sleep?

3. Read 1 John 2:16 and then 2 Samuel 11:2-4. What is the pattern David followed in both of these passages?

4. How did David try to cover up his actions?

5. Who is Nathan?

6. How did Nathan point out David's actions?

7. According to verses 13, how did David respond to Nathan's story?

8. What happened to the child?

9. What consequences did Nathan predict concerning David and his household?

10. What do you think was at the heart of David's depression? (See also Psalm 32 and Psalm 51)

11. Record what you learned from this passage before going to the next passage.

Read 1 Kings 18-19 and answer the following questions.

1. Who is Elijah?

2. Who was looking for Elijah and why?

3. What instruction did Elijah give to Ahab in verse 19?

4. In verse 21, what question did Elijah ask?

5. Did the people answer him?

6. What challenge did Elijah offer to them?

7. What did these prophets do to get their god to answer them?

8. How long did they act this way?

9. What did Elijah do to insure that the answer would truly be from God?

10. What things happened after God showed himself to be the real God?

11. When Elijah knew Jezebel was going to kill him, what did he do?

12. According to verse 4, what did he say?

13. *What things took place on the Mount Horeb that Elijah witnessed?*

14. *Was God in those special events?*

15. *In verse 13, what does Elijah hear?*

16. *Does Elijah change his tune when questioned by God? (See verses 10 and 14).*

17. *What do you think was at the heart of Elijah's depression?*

In all four biblical examples, what was the root of these men's depression? Carefully explain your response.

Depression is a wrong response to life. rkt

Consider the following verses and record how they would help a person suffering from depression.

- *Lamentations 3:16-24*

- *Psalm 77*

- *1 Peter 5:6-7*

- *Psalm 147:3*

- *Psalm 42:5, 11*

- *Psalm 43:1*

Here are some action steps for someone experiencing depression.

1. Identify the real source of your depression.

2. Confess to God that you are depending on yourself instead of God.

3. Ask God to help you trust Him.

4. Read your Bible daily.

5. Pray regularly and frequently.

6. Resume your responsibilities

7. Attend church

8. Join a fellowship for friendship and accountability

9. Serve other people

10. Memorize Scripture

Can you make a list of other things someone can do to help alleviate depression?

Picture an old fashion southern mansion. You know the type – the ones with the white colonnades. There are at least six colonnades that must be town down and replaced when someone is experiencing depression. Complete the chart below to begin your journey out of depression.

Tear Down/Put-Off	Built Up/Put-On
WRONG THINKING WHEN I BECOME DEPRESSSED, WHAT AM I THINGKING?	**RIGHT THINKING** WHAT SHOULD I BE THINKING?
A LIFE BASED ON FEELINGS WHEN I BECOME DEPRESSED, WHAT AM I FEELING?	**A LIFE BASED ON FACTS** WHAT ARE THE FACTS ABOUT THE SITUATION I AM FACING
IMPATIENCE WHEN I WAS DEPRESSED, HOW DID I SHOW MY IMPATIENCE?	**WAITING ON GOD** WHAT SPECIFIC WAYS CAN I WAIT ON GOD DURING THIS TIME?

POOR DECISION MAKING WHEN I WAS DEPRESSED IN THE PAST, WHAT DECISIONS DID I MAKE AND WHAT WAS THE OUTCOME OF THOSE DECISIONS?	**A LIFE OF WISDOM** GOD WANTS ME TO LIVE SKILLFULLY DURING THIS TIME. WHAT DOES GOD WANT ME TO DO? WHERE DO I GO TO FIND THE ANSWERS?
IDOLS OF THE EXPERTS WHAT ARE THE DOCTORS, FRIENDS, AND FAMILY TELLING ME ABOUT MY DEPRESSION?	**CHRIST AS SOVEREIGN LORD** WHAT IS CHRIST TELLING ME ABOUT MY DEPRESSION? WHO AM I GOING TO BELIEVE?
OWNERSHIP IN WHAT WAYS AM I DOING WHAT I WANT TO DO BECAUSE I THINK I CAN?	**STEWARDSHIP** WHAT SHOULD I BE DOING WITH MY TIME, TALENTS, AND TREASURES BECAUSE I KNOW THEY BELONG TO GOD, NOT ME?

LESSON 11

I Feel Hopelessness

*Rescue the weak and needy **(Psalm 82:4a)***

"More than any other time in history, humanity faces a crossroads. One path leads to despair and utter hopelessness; the other to total extinction. Let us pray we have the wisdom to choose correctly" (Woody Allen). These are the words of someone who is rich, famous, probably lacks very little, has a degree of respect from his peers, but is hopeless, has no future, and believes that after life is annihilation. Can you imagine living life for the moment? Any tragedy would be nearly unbearable! Allen and others cry out, if they do cry out, to gods that have hands but cannot give; who have feet, but cannot go with them; who have ears, but do not hear them; who have mouths, but do not speak to them (Psalm 115:7).

The child of God cries out to a God who will rescue the weak and needy. The believer will face difficult times. Often these times are harsh, cruel, and relentless. They come in tidal waves, like a tsunami, with all of its force and destruction. Yet, you and I can turn to God in the day of our troubles, and He will rescue us.

Read the following verses. Record how each one can help you when you feel hopeless.

- *Psalm 9:9*

- *Psalm 20:1*

- *Psalm 22:11*

- *Psalm 27:5*

- *Psalm 32:7*

- *Psalm 37:39*

- *Psalm 41:1*

- *Psalm 46:1*

- *Psalm 50:15*

- *Psalm 54:7*

- *Psalm 77:13-15*

- *Psalm 81:7*

- *Psalm 86:7*

- *Psalm 91:14-15*

- *Psalm 107:6, 13, 19, 28*

- *Psalm 120:1*

- *Psalm 138:7*

- *Psalm 143:11*

Read the following verses and finish the phrase, "The Lord is…"

- *Psalm 16:5*

- *Psalm 18:2*

- *Psalm 18:30*

- *Psalm 23:1*

- *Psalm 27:1*

- *Psalm 18:7*

- *Psalm 18:8*

- *Psalm 33:18*

- *Psalm 34:4*

- *Psalm 34:18*

- *Psalm 37:24*

- *Psalm 54:4*

- *Psalm 100:5*

- *Psalm 103:8*

- *Psalm 118:6*

- *Psalm 118:7*

- *Psalm 118:14*

- *Psalm 121:5*

- *Psalm 145:9*

- *Psalm 145:18*

Select 3 to 5 verses from this section. Record a present hopeless situation you are facing. Write out in the space below how these verses can help you fight this feeling of hopelessness and live victoriously.

LESSON 12

I Seem to Have Lost My Purpose in Life

The LORD has made everything for His own purpose **(Proverbs 16:4a)**

Purpose in life and identity go together. They are two different sides of the same coin. What am I suppose to be doing (purpose) and who I am (identity) are mutually inclusive of one another.

For many years, you were a soldier and what you did (your MOS) defined you – it was your identity and purpose. For a number of years my purpose, when I was enlisted, was a military policeman. My purpose varied throughout my career, but nonetheless I was an M.P. That was my purpose. My identity defined me as a sergeant.

I was lost when I was discharged. I was confused. I bounced around. I drifted. I was aimless. I often told people I did not know what I wanted to be when I grew up...and I was in my twenties!

Today, people remain confused, lost, bouncing around, and aimless. They have excelled in college. They secured a fantastic job in their career field. They are climbing the corporate ladder. But they are still lost, confused, and aimless. What does it looks like? They are searching for the next thrill, lack of contentment, dissatisfied, always looking at the greener grass on the other side, seldom sustaining a sense of happiness, and being gnawed on the inside knowing there has got to be something more.

Let's explore what the Bible has to say about the purpose of life and your identity.

Before entering the military, list what were some of your goals in life?

After Re-Entry in life and living, did any of those goals change? If so, which ones and how did they change?

What are you doing now? How do you know for sure this is what you are supposed to be doing?

Take a moment and answer the following question. "Who am I?"

If you were to change your career pathway (purpose) and it was toward an upward mobility, how would that make you feel?

Would you feel you were successful or a failure? Explain your response.

If you were to change your career (purpose) and it was toward a downward mobility, how would that make you feel?

Would you feel you were successful or a failure? Explain your response.

Read Joshua 1:7-8 and answer the following questions.

1. What word is mentioned repeatedly?

2. List what God requires of Joshua?

Do you want to prosper and be successful?

Are you willing to do what God requires of you?

What do you think your success would look like?

There is a basic purpose in life for the child of God. Read the following verses and record what that purpose is.

- *Psalm 86:9, 12*

- *Romans 15:6*

- *1 Corinthians 6:20*

- *1 Peter 4:16*

Read the following verses and record the common theme.

- *Job 1:9*

- *Psalm 66:16*

- *Ecclesiastes 5:7*

- *Ecclesiastes 8:12*

- *Ecclesiastes 12:13*

- *1 Peter 2:17*

Read the following verses and record the believer's identity (who they are) or what God has done for you.

- *Romans 1:7*

- *Romans 12:1*

- *Romans 16:3*

- *Romans 16:5*

- *Romans 12:8*

- *Romans 12:13*

- *1 Corinthians 1:2*

- *Ephesians 1:5*

- *Romans 8:17*

- *Galatians 3:26*

- *Romans 8:33*

- *Ephesians 1:4*

- *Ephesians 1:7*

- *Ephesians 1:13*

- *Ephesians 1:14*

In light of these great truths, Paul says there is a certain lifestyle that God expects from His children. Read the following verses and complete the phrase, "Walk...." It may be a positive command or a negative command (Do not walk...)

- *Romans 6:4*

- *Romans 8:4*

- *2 Corinthians 5:7*

- *Galatians 5:16*

- *Galatians 5:25*

- *Ephesians 4:1*

- *Ephesians 4:17*

- *Ephesians 5:2*

- *Ephesians 5:8*

- *Ephesians 5:15*

- *Colossians 1:10*

- *1 Thessalonians 2:12*

- *1 Thessalonians 4:1*

- *1 John 1:7*

- *2 John 6*

Write down the most significant insights you learned from this lesson.

LESSON 13

I Need Help In Adjusting to Changes in the Family Unit

Not too long ago, I read a copy of a letter of resignation from the president of Steelcase. The third paragraph of that letter to his employees read:

I am leaving Steelcase to put the balance back in my life. Since rejoining the company five and half years ago, the time I have had to devote to family, personal interests and spiritual growth has gradually diminished. I now find the only way to regain that balance is to leave the company and sway the pendulum back the other way. This is the right time for me to do this: I am 43 years old, my children are young, and they will not be young again.

This man's antennas picked up that his life was out of balance and his family was suffering. And he did something about it. – Dr Paul Faulkner, Achieving Success Without Failing Your Family, (Howard Publishing, 1994), p. 139.

Perhaps upon Re-Entry to life and living, you discovered life was out of balance. This would be expected. You shouldn't be surprised that "things" changed while you were gone. You were deployed between 12-15 months. You left behind a dear wife and several children ranging in age. Or your bride was pregnant and you haven't seen or held your new baby. The kids grew up. They matured. They made new friends. Their taste in music, clothing, and food changed. Your wife had to change. She had to assume "command." She made all the decisions. Could your daughter attend this or that overnight? Could one of your children get a part time job? What about that youth group activity? What about curfew? Driver's permit? Lights out? Meals? Family devotions? Repairing the car? Changing the oil? Do we get a new washer and dryer or a rebuild combo? So many different decisions that you were once actively involved with. Even if you were involved while deployed, it was still from a distance and perhaps influenced by your own distractions.

Now you are home. Your presence is welcomed with open arms. Loving gestures are showered upon you. The first few days or weeks are great. Such joy, warmth, and love. But then life returns to normal, the wife and kids seem too scattered, and you are bewildered. What happened to the family solidarity? You begin to hear comments like, "I'm sorry honey. I guess I forgot to tell you." Or, "Gee dad, I always go here on Tuesday evening."

Re-Entry into an existing family structure that changed while you were gone has its own set of unique challenges. However, the biblical structure of the family is timeless. What needs to happen is everyone in the family unit needs a refresher course on what is a family. This will help with adjusting to the changes in the family unit.

Read the following verses and write down what the Bible says about the role of the husband.

- *Proverbs 31:28*

- *1 Corinthians 14:35*

- *Ephesians 5:23*

- *Ephesians 5:24*

- *Ephesians 5:25*

- *Ephesians 5:28*

- *Colossians 3:18*

- *Colossians 3:19*

- *1 Peter 3:7*

Families are like fudge - mostly sweet with a few nuts. ~Author Unknown

Read the following verses and write down what the Bible says about the role of the father.

- *Deuteronomy 4:10*

- *Deuteronomy 6:7*

- *Psalm 103:13*

- *Proverbs 3:12*

- *Proverbs 4:1*

- *Proverbs 6:20*

- *Proverbs 19:18*

- *Proverbs 19:27*

- *Proverbs 23:22*

- *Malachi 2:15*

- *1 Corinthians 7:3-4*

- *Ephesians 5:33*

- *Ephesians 6:4*

- *Colossians 3:21*

- *1 Thessalonians 2:11*

- *Hebrews 12:9*

I don't care how poor a man is; if he has family, he's rich. Anonymous

Read the following verses and write down what the Bible says about the role of the wife.

- *Deuteronomy 4:10*

- *Proverbs 12:4*

- *Proverbs 19:13*

- *Proverbs 19:14*

- *Proverbs 31:10-31*

- *1 Corinthians 7:3-4*

- *1 Corinthians 7:39*

- *Ephesians 5:22*

- *Ephesians 5:24*

- *Ephesians 5:25*

- *Ephesians 5:28*

- *Colossians 3:18*

- *Colossians 3:19*

- *1 Peter 3:1*

- *1 Peter 3:4*

Read the following verses and write down what the Bible says about the role of the mother.

- *Psalm 127:3*

- *Proverbs 6:20*

- *Proverbs 29:15*

- *2 Timothy 1:5*

Read the following verses and write down what the Bible says about the role of children.

- *Psalm 34:11*

- *Psalm 78:5*

- *Proverbs 1:8*

- *Proverbs 1:10*

- *Proverbs 1:15*

- *Proverbs 2:1*

- *Proverbs 3:1*

- *Proverbs 3:11*

- *Proverbs 4:10*

- *Proverbs 4:20*

- *Proverbs 5:1*

- *Proverbs 6:3*

- *Proverbs 6:20*

- *Proverbs 7:1*

- *Proverbs 10:1*

- *Proverbs 10:5*

- *Proverbs 13:1*

- *Proverbs 15:20*

- *Proverbs 17:25*

- *Proverbs 19:13*

- *Proverbs 19:26*

- *Proverbs 19:27*

- *Proverbs 23:15*

- *Proverbs 23:19*

- *Proverbs 23:26*

- *Proverbs 24:21*

- *Proverbs 27:11*

- *Proverbs 28:7*

- *Proverbs 31:28*

- *Ephesians 6:1*

- *Colossians 3:20*

A mother and father decided to use psychology in raising their children. For example, at bedtime they would say to the children, "Would you like to take your doll to bed or your teddy bear to bed?" You see, the beauty of this is that in either case the child is choosing to go to bed. But the whole system collapsed when the three- year-old, who was never allowed to go out after supper, said to her parents one evening, "Do you want me to go out the back door or should I go out the front?"

In light of this information, use this page and take a stab at drawing a diagram that would show clearly, what the family structure would look like biblically. Develop your diagram so it can be a teaching tool for your family and others.

LESSON 14

How Do I Restore and Renew Communication with My Family?

*Like apples of gold in settings of silver is a word spoken in right circumstances (**Proverbs 25:11**)*

What type of communication did you experience in the military? Your first experience was with the recruiter. He was nice, pleasant, and cheerful. You enlisted, completed the medical exams, caught the transport to your training base, and were greeted by your Drill Sergeant. Culture shock! He/she was nothing like the cheerful recruiter. He yelled, screamed, he stomped, he raved, and he didn't even smile!

You completed your basic training and you're A.I.T. You received orders for your new assignment. I think King Solomon might have summarized your new base and its communication style when he penned, "Nothing new under the sun."

So for many ever years you have served our country faithfully, your re-entry into life and living – your communication is under great strain. Do you find yourself speaking to your wife and children like that Drill Sergeant? Or your C.O.? Or the battalion commander? You think you are communicating well, but those who hear you complain that you are barking out orders like you are back on the base! They say, "We're not your soldier dad (honey)! Treat us with respect!"

Re-Entry into life and living affects how you communicate. There is a verse in the Bible that says, "The wise in heart will be called understanding, and sweetness of speech increases persuasiveness." (Proverbs 16:21)

This study is designed to help you examine your communication patterns and help you make improvements as you recognize the need. So, let's begin.

Make a list of what you think are the greatest hindrances to communication in your family. For example:

1. They don't seem to listen to me when I speak…

2. _____

3. _____

4. _____

5. _____

6. _____

7. _____

8. _____

9. _____

10. _____

Consult a good dictionary and write out the definition for communication.

Effective communication is the process of sharing information with another person in such a way that the sender's message is understood as he/she intended it. Unless the sender and the receiver have come to a common meaning, they haven't communicated effectively.

Read Ephesians 4:23 and Philippians 2:1-3. When people communicate effectively, it will result in:

1) *Mutual strengthening. What would this look like?*

2) *Mutual encouraging. What would this look like?*

3) *Mutual enriching. What would this look like?*

Read Ephesians 4:23 and Philippians 2:1-3. What do these verses say about good communication?

What are the three forms of communication?

1._____

2._____

3._____

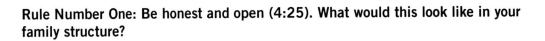

Read Ephesians 4:25-32. There are four rules that can increase the effectiveness of your communication. I will list them along with the verses. What you need to do is explain the rule and provide an example of what this would look like in your family structure.

Rule Number One: Be honest and open (4:25). What would this look like in your family structure?

Rule Number Two: Keep short accounts (4:26-27). Explain what this would look like?

Rule Number Three: Attack the problem, not the person (4:29). Describe the last time you attacked the person. What were the results? If you could replay the situation using attack the problem, what would that look like? Would the outcome be different? How?

Rule Number Four: Act, don't react (4:31-32). What is your typical reaction? What types of actions should you have?

One of the chief hindrances to good communication is non-verbal cues. Make a list of non-verbal cues that hinder effective communication. An example would be

- *Someone folding their arms across their chest*

- _____

- _____

- _____

- _____

- _____

- _____

- _____

Think back on your most recent communication problem. Answer each of the following questions to see how it would have changed how you spoke to the other person.

1. Did you think about the person that you were going to speak to?

2. Did you think through the topic that you were going to talk to the person in light of knowing them?

3. Did you think through the person's possible objections?

4. Did you think through what approach you would take to talk to the person?

5. Did you think through the words that you were going to say?

6. Did you consider when to speak to this person?

7. Did you think through your goal of talking to this person?

Did you know we communicate more non-verbally than we do verbally? Non-verbal messages are powerful. Below are key truths about non-verbal communication. After reading each statement, write a few sentences explaining the concept.

- *Create your own environment*

- *Know what others see in you*

- *Keep in touch with yourself*

- *Know when to explain*

- *Interpret others actions carefully*

Learn to use communication to clarify. Ask questions such as

1. Help me understand...
2. What do you mean by...
3. Is this what you're saying...
4. Let me summarize...

Add at least three more clarifying questions you could use to improve your communication skills.

Communication is a two-way street. It requires both sending and receiving messages. The listener is just as important as the speaker. The importance of being a good listener can hardly be over estimated. Listening is important to God. Therefore, it must be important to us.

Write out an explanation for the following phrase. "Listening with your outer man."

Write out an explanation for the following phrase. "Listening with your inner man."

Read each of the following verses and write out the type of speech (words) you should avoid.

- *Proverbs 4:24*

- *Proverbs 19:1*

- *Ecclesiastes 5:6*

- *Proverbs 2:16*

- *Proverbs 10:19*

- *Proverbs 14:7*

- *Proverbs 16:27*

- *Proverbs 18:8*

- *Proverbs 26:22*

- *Proverbs 29:22*

- *Ecclesiastes 6:11*

- *Proverbs 15:1*

Read each of the following verses and write out the type of speech (words) you should use.

- *Proverbs 16:21*

- *Proverbs 17:7*

- *Proverbs 22:11*

- *Proverbs 12:14*

- *Proverbs 15:26*

- *Proverbs 16:24*

- *Proverbs 17:27*

- *Proverbs 18:4*

- *Ecclesiastes 7:21*

- *Ecclesiastes 9:17*

- *Ecclesiastes 10:12*

- *Proverbs 8:6*

- *Proverbs 23:16*

- *Ecclesiastes 3:7*

- *Proverbs 15:23*

- *Proverbs 25:11*

- *Ecclesiastes 5:2*

Communication is the best tool to resolve conflict. Some people will <u>fight</u> to win a conflict. Some people will <u>flee</u> to avoid the conflict. Some people with <u>fight</u> and then <u>flee</u>. Which one(s) do you use to win a conflict?

Some people believe they must win the argument. Others believe they will lose. Some will resign, while others will compromise. Take each of the bolded words and describe what this would look like when two people are fighting.

Here is a general matrix for resolving conflicts. Memorize the principle and then read the Scriptures. Then reflect on your last conflict and write out what you will do differently in the future.

1. *Have I chosen words that would invite the other person to respond to me? Read Proverbs 12:25, 15:23, and 16:23.*

2. *Do I have all the facts? Read Proverbs 18:13.*

3. *Have I chosen the proper time to discuss the problem? Read Proverbs 15:23, 28; 25:11-12*

4. *Am I mindful of my non-verbal communication style?*

5. How will I acknowledge my involvement in initiating or fostering the problem?

6. Am I open-minded or closed-minded toward this person?

7. Do I have the right attitude? Read Ephesians 4:15, 32.

8. Am I willing to admit my culpability? Read Genesis 8:8-19; Proverbs 20:6

9. Am I willing to change? Read John 5:6; Matthew 5:23-26

10. Am I willing to act responsible no matter how I feel? Read Galatians 6:5; James 1:13-15

11. *Am I willing to stay on task and deal with one problem at a time? Read Matthew 6:34*

12. *Am I willing to avoid retaliation if the results do not favor me? Read Romans 12:18-20*

Space to write additional insights.

How few there are who have the courage enough to own their faults, or resolution enough to mend them. — Benjamin Franklin

LESSON 15

How Do I Establish New Goals for Re-Entry

The vision must be followed by the venture.
It is not enough to stare up the steps - we must step up the stairs.
~Vance Havner

The rung of a ladder was never meant to rest upon, but only to hold a
man's foot long enough to enable him to put the other somewhat higher.
~Thomas Henry Huxley

Vision without action is a daydream.
Action without vision is a nightmare.   ~Japanese Proverb

Re-Entry. Life has changed but I can live life. This means that an honest evaluation of what you want is required. Many of the inspirational quotes on *goals* speak of action, not apathy; of doing, not sitting; involvement and participation, not warming the bench or being an armchair quarterback.

Everyone in life needs goals. Without goals, a person flounders aimlessly. This can result in frustration, anger, despair, and depression. Life can become meaningless. A person without goals often merely exists; they lack joy, and cannot see any clear hope for the future.

The military branch you so faithfully served for the past several years set your goals. Now Re-Entry into life and living is a reality. You can select your own clothing; no more camouflaged fatigues or dress blues. So what were your goals before you enlisted? Were you in the middle of an educational program? Were you part of a company with a bright future? Did you own your own business? Do you want to return to those goals? While in the service, did something different spark your interest? Did you receive specialized training while in the military that you think you might like to pursue now that you are discharged? I remember considering becoming a law enforcement officer because I enjoyed my years as a Military Policeman. That desire never materialized. I lacked goals.

Consider the following verses and record what they say about goals or aims.

- *Psalm 4:2*

- *1 Corinthians 9:26-27*

- *Luke 13:32*

- *Philippians 3:14*

- *1 Timothy 1:5*

As you consider your goals, whether revised or new, look at your goals honestly. Some people fail to reach their goal because the goal appears cumbersome. The goal itself is great, but it is like asking an infant to bite off a piece of rare "T" bone steak. Many times the goal needs to be broken down into smaller steps.

For example, if you became interested in airplane mechanics, and you want to become a master technician, you need to think, and perhaps get advice, what precise steps you need to take to accomplish that goal. Do you need more education? What schools are available in your area to continue your education? Would you have to relocate to receive training? What employment opportunities are available as a student for "hand's-on experience?" If employed, will the new employer pay for continuing education? These questions, as well as others, can provide a sense of reassurance and perseverance toward that goal, or help you refine your goal, or perhaps guide you toward another related goal.

How do I set goals? First, whatever goals you set should be reasonable, attainable, and measurable. Nothing is impossible, but some goals are unrealistic. A goal is the will of God for a specific area of my life, that when implemented, will bring honor and glory to God. Goals can relate to the physical, emotional, mental, social, intellectual, financial, or spiritual areas of your life.

To begin the goal setting procedure, write out succinctly your stated goal. Try to write out the goal in a single sentence. Make the sentence clear and concise. Practice by writing out a goal using the space below.

Second, anticipate the who's, what's, where's, when's, how's, or why's that may hinder your achieving the stated goal. Just because you establish a goal does not mean it will come to past. A goal is the end-product. You must exert great effort, patience, fortitude, and determination to achieve the goal. Along the way, you will encounter obstacles. The more you can anticipate the obstacles the greater probability you have for reaching your goal. Using the goal you wrote out, list the potential obstacles that would hinder you from reaching that goal.

Third, these are possible ways that you can eliminate, avoid, and manage the anticipated obstacles. Every obstacle has a solution. If I have the goal of rising thirty minutes earlier to exercise, and you know one of the obstacles you might face is hitting the snooze alarm, what can you do to avoid doing that and reach your goal of getting up thirty minutes earlier. For each of the obstacles you listed above, write down several things you could do to overcome it. Be specific and realistic.

Finally, goals often change. Sometimes your circumstances will affect your goals. Unforeseeable events can affect you accomplishing your goals. A number of things can occur that will seem to frustrate you in your pursuits. Remember a very important truth. Oftentimes those things that alter your course are out of your control. People's decisions or plans can affect you. You were not consulted. Their choices might escalate your plans or may delay those plans. But more importantly, as a believer, although it is out of your control, nothing that touches your life is out of God's control. Read the following Scriptures that speak of God being in control.

- *Psalm 24:1*

- *Proverbs 16:4*

- *Revelation 4:11*

- *Psalm 47:4*

- *1 Chronicles 29:11*

There are goal setting work sheets on the next several pages. Feel free to make copies of this form. Use them often. Refer to them frequently. Review your goals often. Make adjustments as necessary. Remain focused. Work hard. Seek God. Seek to accomplish the goal for God's glory. Then it will be beneficial to you and those who surround you.

_____ Goal
(Type of goal: Spiritual, mental, family, financial, etc.)

_____

Write out your goal in a sentence.

I want to reach this goal by: _____
                                    Set a reasonable date. Be realistic.

Below are possible obstacles I may encounter toward my goal

1. _____

2. _____

3. _____

Below are possible solutions I can use to meet the obstacles so I can proceed toward my goal.

1. _____

2. _____

3. _____

_____ Goal
(Type of goal: Spiritual, mental, family, financial, etc.)

_____
Write out your goal in a sentence.

I want to reach this goal by _____
Set a reasonable date. Be realistic.

Below are possible obstacles I may encounter toward my goal

1. _____

2. _____

3. _____

Below are possible solutions I can use to meet the obstacles so I can proceed toward my goal.

1. _____

2. _____

3. _____

_____ Goal
(Type of goal: Spiritual, mental, family, financial, etc.)

_____

Write out your goal in a sentence.

I want to reach this goal by _____

                                 Set a reasonable date. Be realistic.

Below are possible obstacles I may encounter toward my goal

1. _____

2. _____

3. _____

Below are possible solutions I can use to meet the obstacles so I can proceed toward my goal.

1. _____

2. _____

3. _____

133

LESSON 16

In a Crowd but Lonely

*Turn to me and be gracious to me, for I am lonely
and afflicted* **(Psalm 25:16)**

Right now, you might be confused. Why am I experiencing what I am experiencing? Let me see if I understand what you might be going through. You had to deal with separation from your family, relatives, and friends when you were first deployed. You wondered how you would make it without them being close by. The initial hours turned into days, then weeks, and then months, perhaps years. It is not as if you forgot them, but you became wrapped up in your responsibilities. But something else occurred. Your platoon became your family. They were always around. Together you went out on missions. You had each other's backs. They were your safety net. You relied upon them. There was a silent bond and commitment. You laughed, cried, and played card games. You hung out together. You may have even taken some R & R together.

As your tour was ending, your thoughts were reignited to family, relatives, and friends. Fond memories of holidays, birthdays, and celebrations were rekindled in your mind as you counted the days to return home. Preparations were made to welcome you home. But as you stood among your family, relatives, and friends, you experienced a real sense of loneliness. It is a strange feeling. Some notice that you seem withdrawn. You want to be by yourself a lot of the time. Those close to you ask, "What is wrong?" You try to explain but they don't seem to understand. After a while, you get tired of trying to explain. This causes discomfort. Those close to you feel like you are pushing them away. This is not your intention, but your emotions are all over the map.

Re-entry into relationships is often difficult for many of our nation's finest. It is not a deliberate choice. It is a result of living with a form of isolation. Yes, you were surrounded by your buddies, while those nearest and dearest to you were thousands of miles away. Weekly telephone calls, daily e-mails, and frequent care packages don't cut it. Shop talk, details for the upcoming mission, and the focus on survival occupied your thoughts.

So what can you do when you are in a crowd and feel lonely?

Let's construct a logical presentation for you. First, make a list of all the reasons you can think of for why you feel lonely. Spend some time really thinking about this as you make your list.

Loneliness is a feeling, something someone experiences. Loneliness is traced to a trust issue. While serving you had to trust my comrades. Daily living was the theater in which trust was tested and proved. The gunner in your vehicle, the point man on the trail, or the radio personnel became the resources of surviving another day.

Eliminating loneliness begins with a focus on what are the real facts. Loneliness thrives on feelings, past experiences, and "what was." As the title of this study suggests, someone can be in a crowd and still feel lonely. They can count the number of people, reaffirm their relationship to each one, but still experience a sense of loneliness. Feelings must surrender to facts. What does the Bible say about loneliness? Read the following verses and record the significant insights.

God created man to be a social creature. What does Genesis 2:15-24 say?

Read Ruth 1. What commitment does Ruth make to Naomi? (In-laws)

Read 2 Kings 2:2, 4, 6. What commitment does Elisha make to Elijah? (Friends)

Read Matthew 26:56. What happened to Jesus?

Read 2 Timothy 4:9-11. What happened to Paul?

What comfort do the following verses provide you?

- *Genesis 28:15*

- *Joshua 1:5*

- *Joshua 1:9*

- *1 Chronicles 28:20*

- *John 14:18*

- *Hebrews 13:5*

What does Proverbs 18:24 say?

Read Ephesians 5:22-6:4. This passage speaks of relationships. What do all of these relationships have in common? What is the common thread? What significance does this common thread have to help you in your relationships and loneliness?

Loneliness, for those Re-entering life and living, is rooted in trust. Often, after a tour of duty, you only trust those in your unit. And at times, even those in your unit did not earn the right to be trusted. They were "goof-off's." The Christian only has one person they can unreservedly trust, One who is constant and always faithful, One who keeps His word, and One who will not let you down. Consider the following verses and what they say about this One.

- *Deuteronomy 7:9*

- *Isaiah 49:7*

- *Romans 8:38-39*

- *1 Corinthians 1:9*

- *1 Corinthians 10:13*

- *2 Corinthians 1:18*

- *1 Thessalonians 5:24*

- *2 Thessalonians 3:3*

- *2 Timothy 2:13*

- *1 Peter 4:19*

- *1 John 1:9*

- *Revelation 19:11*

Now examine these verses and remember how near and dear of a Friend is Jesus. Write a sentence on how God's faithfulness to you can help you when you feel lonely.

I will bless Thee, Genesis 12:2

I will not fail Thee, Joshua 1:5

I will heal Thee, 2 Kings 20:5

I will instruct Thee, Psalm 32:8

I will teach Thee, Psalm 32:8

I will deliver Thee, Psalm 50:15

I will satisfy Thee, Psalm 132:15

I will help Thee, Isaiah 41:10

I will strengthen Thee, Isaiah 41:10

I will uphold Thee, Isaiah 41:10

I will hold Thine hand, Isaiah 42:6

I will not forget Thee, Isaiah 49:15

I will comfort Thee, Isaiah 66:13

I will forgive, Jeremiah 31:34

I will restore, Jeremiah 30:17

I will be your God, Ezekiel 36:28

I will put my Spirit within you, Ezekiel 36:27

I will save you, Ezekiel 36:27, 29

I will love him, John 14:21

I will manifest myself, John 14:21

I will come again, John 14:3

I will sup with him, Revelation 3:20

I will give Thee a crown of life, Revelation 2:10

Let a man go away or come back: God never leaves.
He is always at hand and if he cannot get into your life,
still he is never farther away than the door. – Meister Eckhart (C. 1260–
C. 1327)

An old seaman said, "In fierce storms we can do but one thing. There
is only one way (to survive); we must put the ship in a certain position
and keep her there."

Commenting on this idea, Richard Fuller wrote:

This, Christian, is what you must do. Sometimes, like Paul, you can see neither sun nor stars, and no small tempest lies on you. Reason cannot help you. Past experiences give you no light. Only a single course is left. You must stay upon the Lord; and come what may – winds, waves, cross seas, thunder, lightning, frowning rocks, roaring breakers – no matter what, you must lash yourself to the helm and hold fast your confidence in God's faithfulness and his everlasting love in Christ Jesus.

My friend, you are never alone. If you feel you can't trust anyone, YOU CAN trust the Lord. Go back and re-read all of the verses that God wrote to you. Memorize ones that are meaningful to you. Look at all the faithful family relationships you studied about in this lesson. In the space below, write out a prayer of thanksgiving for Jesus, the Friend that sticks closer than a brother, and all who love and surround you.

Dear God…

LESSON 17

Dealing with Stress

Apart from such external things,
there is the daily pressure on me of concern for all the
churches (2 Corinthians 11:28)

Everyone has stress. Everyone deals with stress. Stress is part of everyday life. There is no escaping it. Every day has some type of stress. Even the one who says they don't get stressed but give stress to others must deal with stress. Stress is inevitable. Stress can be internal and external. The question is not whether our lives will be touched by stress, but what we do when stress does touch our loves.

> Everyone experiences problems. Reverend Norman Vincent Peale tells of a time he was walking down the street in New York City when he ran into an old friend, George. "Norman, I'm fed up," George announced. "I have nothing but problems, problems, problems. I'd give you $5,000 right now if you could get rid of all my problems." Norman ruminated for a minute and then replied, "Just yesterday I was in a place where there were a lot of people with no problems. Would you like to go?" George pounced on the offer. "Good," Peale answered. "Tomorrow afternoon, I'll take you to the Westchester cemetery. The only people who don't have problems are dead." – Erik Olesen, "Mastering Change," Success Magazine, October 1993

Stress often involves change. Many people view stress as negative. Stress is a response to your environment. Stress is related to perceived or actual imbalance. Stress is a response to demands placed upon us by others or yourself.

One type of stress is survival stress. This occurs when your survival or health is threatened, where you are put under pressure, or where you experience some unpleasant or challenging event. Here adrenaline is released in your body and you experience all the symptoms of your body preparing for fight or flight.

Internally generated stress can come from anxious worrying about events beyond your control, from a tense, hurried approach to life, or from relationship problems caused by your own behavior.

Stress is harmful physically, emotionally, mentally, and spiritually. Stress can affect your digestive, immune, nervous, and cardiovascular systems. Stress can affect your relationships. It can affect your work and productivity. Stress can even cause more stress!

> Let's define stress as "the feeling I have toward situations that appear to be overwhelming in my judgment."

There are two words in the Bible that deal with your stress. Those words are rest and peace.

Read the following verses and record how rest is pictured or described.

Exodus 33:14; 2 Samuel 7:11; Matthew 11:28.

God says I will _____ you rest.

Deuteronomy 12:10; Joshua 1:13

God says He _____ you rest

Joshua 22:4

God _____ _____ you rest.

Joshua 23:1

The Lord _____ _____ you rest.

144

Joshua 21:44; 2 Samuel 7:1; 1 Kings 5:4; 1 Chronicles 22:18; 2 Chronicles 14:7, 15:15

God _____ rest on every side

Exodus 31:14, 34:12, 21

The Bible says there is a _____ rest.

Leviticus 16:31

The Bible says there is a _____ rest.

Hebrews 4:1-12

You must _____ into His rest

Jeremiah 45:3; Lamentations 1:3

The Bible is equally frank and honest that there are those who _____ ____ rest.

Deuteronomy 28:65

And there are those who find _____ rest.

Read Matthew 11:28-30 and answer the following questions.

- *What is the first word in verse 28? What imagery comes to mind?*

- *Who are being invited?*

- *Describe someone who is weary and heavy laden.*

- *What does Jesus promise to them?*

- *What two things must this type of person do?*

- *What is a "yoke?"*

- *What things should this type of person "learn" about Jesus?*

- *How does Jesus describe Himself?*

- *What promise does Jesus repeat?*

- *How does Jesus describe His yoke and burden?*

- *What do you have to do to receive the promise He is offering?*

Peace is the second word the Bible says that deals with stress. Rest is external while peace is internal. Read the following passages and record what they say about peace.

Deuteronomy 20:10

There are _____ of peace.

Ezra 9:12

There is a _____ of peace to be avoided

Psalm 29:11; Psalm 85:8; Ezekiel 37:26

The Lord _____ peace

Psalm 34:14

We are commanded to _____ peace

Proverbs 16:7

Even when opposed by people, God _____ me peace

Isaiah 32:17

Doing the right things _____ peace

Isaiah 54:10

God's promise of peace is _____ .

Jeremiah 14:19, 8:15, 12:12

No peace comes apart from God and His _____ .

Mark 5:34; Luke 7:50, 8:48; Romans 5:1

_____ is a prerequisite for peace

John 14:27

God's offer of peace is so totally different from the _____ offer of peace.

Romans 8:6

What we set out _____ on can bring peace or remove peace.

Romans 16:20

God has my stress under _____ .

Galatians 5:22

Peace is the work of the _____ _____ .

Philippians 4:7

Biblical peace transcends all of our _____ .

Colossians 3:15

I must allow peace to _____ my heart

1 Thessalonians 5:23

God's peace results in _____ and _____ .

Read Psalm 32: 3-4

What caused David's stress?

When you begin to experience stress, consult trusted advisors. Read the following verses and record what they say about counsel from friends.

- *Proverbs 17:17*

- *Proverbs 17:26*

- *Proverbs 27:9*

Vance Havner, a Baptist evangelist, related the story of an elderly lady who was greatly disturbed by her many troubles both real and imaginary. Finally, she was told in a kindly way by her family, "Grandma, we've done all we can do for you. You'll just have to trust God for the rest."

A look of utter despair spread over her face as she replied, "Oh, dear, has it come to that?" Havner commented, "It always comes to that, so we might as well begin with that!"

The following matrix can guide you successfully through the next stressful experience.

EXTERNAL STRESS

- Can I do anything about the stress without violating God's Word?

- If I cannot, then I must examine the lives of Joseph, Daniel and Jesus to learn how they lived victoriously in the mist of very difficult times

- Is this stress a result of sinful actions?

- If it is, then I must comply with biblical confession and repentance

- Is this stress the result of someone else under pressure, which I am serving underneath?

- Read and implement Luke 6, which lists the activities a Christian is commanded to perform when living under the stressful actions of an enemy.

- Am I assuming responsibilities for a situation outside of my control?

- Live under the authority of a good, gracious, and loving God affirming His sovereign control in which He desires to work out all things.

- Is this stress attributed to another's expectations or demands of me? Are these demands reasonable?

- Remind yourself of the Christian's authority, biblical submission, the biblical appeal process (see Daniel and Esther) and choose whom you will serve.

Internal Stress

- Is this stress attributed to laziness or slothfulness?

- Plan your day. Use a Time Scheduler for activities. Understand the purpose for living and work. Redeem the time for the days are evil

- Is this stress attributed to hidden or unconfessed sin?

- Repent, return, and repeat godly attitudes and actions

Emotional Factors

- Am I angry or have unresolved conflicts with someone?

- Am I concerned about what someone may think of me?

- Am I worried about something?

Physical Factors

- What are my diet patterns?

- What are my sleep patterns?

- What are my exercise patterns

- Has there been a recent illness?

- Am I consuming to much artificial stimuli as a coping device? Has food or beverage become comfort food to me?

Spiritual Factors

- Am I in the Word daily?

- Am I praying daily?

- Am I accountable?

- Have I slacked off in Christian service?

- Who are my companions?

No man should be pitied because every day of his life he faces a hard, stubborn problem. It is the man who has no problems to solve, no hardships to face, who is to be pitied. He has nothing in his life, which will strengthen and form his character, nothing to call out his latent powers and deepen and widen his hold on life. – Booker T. Washington

God never gives strength for tomorrow, or for the next hour, but only for the strain of the moment.... The saint is hilarious when he is crushed with difficulties because the thing is so ludicrously impossible to anyone but God. – Oswald Chambers (1874–1917)

LESSON 18

Dealing with Personal Loss

Jesus wept (John 11:35)

Every person will deal with loss. It is inevitable. It may be the loss of a family pet, losing contact with a really neat relative or friend, loss of mobility because of injury, or loss of life. Part of loss is grieving. Jesus lost a very near and dear friend named Lazarus. Lazarus often entertained Jesus and His disciples. Lazarus was Mary and Martha's brother (John 11:1-3, 35). Jesus, the God-man, was familiar with loss, grief, and tears. He understands your loss. In fact, He lost fellowship with His father when the weight of sin crushed Him. He said, "My God, my God, why have you forsaken me?" (Mark 15:34)

There are several factors involved that you must consider when working through your sense of loss. I will pose them in the form of questions. Before looking at how the Bible provides hope for your sorrow, take a few minutes and honestly answer the following questions.

1. *Was the loss part of the natural life expectancy? (age, health factors, terminal illness)*

2. *Was the loss due to a tragic event like a car accident, violence, natural environmental causes (hurricane, tornados, fire, flooding, 911, drive-by)?*

3. Was the loss due to military engagement?

4. Was there anything you truly believe you could have done to prevent this loss? If so, exactly what?

5. Could your actions really prevent the death of this person?

6. How could your actions prevent the person from dying?

In the space provided below, write down your thoughts about how you view death.

People have a variety of viewpoints on death. Some view death as the cessation of life. Others believe that there is life after death. Still others fear death because of the unknowns. Some experience great resignation because life will not be the same without that person.

The authors of the Bible wrote much on death, dying and grief. There are over 460 verses alone on death. Look up each verse and record how the author viewed death.

- *Psalm 116:3, 5*

- *Psalm 23:4*

- *Philippians 1:21-23*

- *2 Corinthians 5:6-8*

- *Job 1:13-22 (especially note what happened to Job and then his response in verses 20-22)*

- *Psalm 34:15*

- *Psalm 55:22*

- *Psalm 57:1-2*

- *Psalm 103:13*

- *2 Corinthians 4:16-18*

Where is Christ in the mist of your grief, sorrow, and loss? Read the following Scriptures and record what they say.

- *Psalm 143:3, 8*

- *Isaiah 61:1-3*

- *2 Corinthians 1:3-4*

- *Psalm 17:15*

- *Psalm 18:2*

- *Psalm 27:13*

- *Deuteronomy 33:27*

- *Psalm 34:15*

- *Psalm 55:22*

- *Isaiah 66:13*

- *John 14:27*

- *Psalm 56:8*

Was Jesus touched by grief, sorrow, and loss? Study the following verses and record how Jesus experienced loss and what you can learn from His example.

- *Isaiah 53:3*

- *Hebrews 4:15-16*

- *Luke 17:11-13*

- *2 Timothy 4:7-8*

- *Revelation 14:13*

Does the Bible offer any reason for someone having to die? For the believer, look at the following verse and record what it says. Notice the "exchange" process.

- *1 Corinthians 15:53-57*

- *Psalm 139:16*

> Jesus Christ alone is qualified to guide us into the vast unknown. Since he is the only one who has returned from the grave, he tells us accurately about life after death. – Erwin W. Lutzer (1941–)

Take special note of 1 Thessalonians 4:11-18. Answer the following questions.

1. What was Paul's desire for these dear people according to verse 13?

2. Why do you think Paul uses the phrase "those who are asleep" to describe death?

3. Does Paul indicate grieving is acceptable for the Christian who has lost someone?

4. According to verse 13, how should a Christian grieve?

5. How does Christ's death and resurrection give hope?

6. According to Paul, who also comes with Christ when He returns for the living?

7. Do those living have an advantage over those who have died?

8. Read verses 16-17. List the order of events Paul describes.

9. In your own words, how could this passage provide hope for you and others?

Take a few minutes and record additional insights you have learned.

By all standards, death is the most dreaded event. Our society will pay any price to prolong life. Just one more month, or even another day. Perhaps our desire to postpone death reflects our dissatisfaction with God's ultimate purpose. Remember, his work isn't finished until we are glorified. Most of us would like to see God's work remain half finished. We're glad we are called and justified, but we're not too excited about being glorified. – Erwin W. Lutzer (1941–)

LESSON 19

What Can I Do To Keep Peace of God?

You shall love the LORD your God with all your heart and with all your soul and with all your might (Deuteronomy 6:5)

Perhaps by now, one could begin to conclude that PTSD is a mindset. It's how we think about what we have seen or witnessed. The event that troubles you might have occurred recently, or you may be struggling with it for some time. Below is 2 Timothy 1:7. Read it at least 5 times, slowly and carefully; taking in each word, thinking about the meaning of this verse. Then answer the questions below the verse.

For God has not given us a spirit of timidity, but of power and love and discipline.

1. The verse begins with a negative. What has God NOT GIVEN you?

2. The verse closes with a positive. What has God GIVEN you?

Read the verse below and answer the following questions.

> And the peace of God, which surpasses all comprehension,
> will guard your hearts and your minds in Christ Jesus (Philippians 4:7)

1. How is the peace of God described?

2. What two areas of your life will the peace of God guard?

3. What do you think "in Christ Jesus" means with reference to this guarding peace?

The rest of this lesson is devoted to showing you how you can have the peace of God. The peace of God is based on having a relationship with the Peace-Giver, Jesus Christ. In Lesson One, we spent time discussing how to have peace with God, or stated differently, how to enter into a real relationship with God. Once you are in that relationship, it is vital to maintain it. If you ignore a human relationship, it is lifeless and meaningless. In the same way, your spiritual relationship to Jesus can suffer if you ignore Him. He is a real Person who longs to walk and talk with you. But you have to want to walk and talk with Him also.

The first thing you can do to maintain your relationship to Jesus is to let Him speak to you. You do this by reading the Bible, His Word. Read the following verses and write down important truths you learn about the Bible.

- *Psalm 18:30*

- *Psalm 33:4*

- *Psalm 33:6*

- *Psalm 119:9*

- *Psalm 119:11*

- *Psalm 119:16*

- *Psalm 119:17*

- *Psalm 119:25*

- *Psalm 119:28*

- *Psalm 119:42*

- *Psalm 119:49*

- *Psalm 119:50*

- *Psalm 119:67*

- *Psalm 119:76*

- *Psalm 119:81*

- *Psalm 119:101*

- *Psalm 119:105*

- *Psalm 119:107*

- *Psalm 119:116*

- *Psalm 119:140*

John Huffman tells the classic story of the man who was in a difficult situation, and in desperation turns to the Bible. He didn't know where to look, so he let the book flop open and he laid his finger on a verse, which said that Judas "went and hanged himself." After a moment's thought, he decided to turn to a different verse for help; he repeated the process and read, "What thou doest, do quickly." Too many of us are "hunt and poke" Bible students, and it's no wonder we have so little understanding of God's Word for us. The Bible requires and deserves our serious attention and study.

Read the following verses and record what descriptions are used for the Bible. Write a few sentences explaining how this description can help you grow closer to God.

- *Psalm 19:10*

- *Psalm 119:103*

- *Hebrews 5:13*

- *1 Peter 2:2*

- *Psalm 119:130*

- *Jeremiah 23:29*

Read the following verses and record how you should respond when you read or hear God's Word.

- *Psalm 81:13*

- *Isaiah 46:12*

- *Mark 7:14*

- *Jeremiah 2:31*

- *Jeremiah 13:15*

- *Romans 10:16*

- *James 1:23*

- *James 1:25*

The second way to maintain your relationship to God is to talk to Him. This is called praying. Read the following verses and note what they have to say about praying.

- *Psalm 5:3*

- *Psalm 17:1*

- *Psalm 32:6*

- *Psalm 69:13*

- *Proverbs 15:29*

- *Romans 12:12*

- *Philippians 4:6*

- *Colossians 4:2*

- *1 Thessalonians 5:17*

Mrs. Oswald Chambers once said of her husband, "Like all teachers of forceful personality, he constantly had people longing to pour out their intimate troubles to him. I remember at the close of one meeting a woman came up to him with the words, "Oh, Mr. Chambers, I feel I must tell you about myself.' As he led her away to a quiet corner, I resigned myself to a long wait; but he was back again in a few minutes. As we went home, I remarked on the speed with which he managed to free himself, and he replied, "I just asked her if she had ever told God all about herself. When she said she hadn't, I advised her to go home and pour out before Him as honestly as she could all her troubles, then see if she still needed or wanted to relate them to me.'" Chambers knew the importance of going directly to Jesus when faced with a special need or a trying situation.

The third area that will build your relationship to God is meditation. Read these verses and note what they say about meditation.

- *Joshua 1:8*

- *Psalm 63:6*

- *Psalm 77:6*

- *Psalm 77:12*

- *Psalm 119:27*

- *Psalm 119:148*

- *Psalm 143:5*

John R. W. Stott once admitted the truth that many of us have felt but failed to confess: "The thing I know will give me the deepest joy – namely, to be alone and unhurried in the presence of God, aware of His presence, my heart open to worship Him – is often the thing I least want to do."

A fourth area is worship. Read these verses and note what they say about worship.

- *Deuteronomy 6:13*

- *Psalm 2:11*

- *Psalm 66:4*

- *Psalm 95:6*

- *Romans 12:1*

- *Revelation 4:10*

Use this space to write down other additional insights you learned.

Worship is the highest and noblest act that any person can do. When men worship, God is satisfied! And when you worship, you are fulfilled! Think about this: why did Jesus Christ come? He came to make worshipers out of rebels. We who were once self-centered have to be completely changed so that we can shift our attention outside of ourselves and become able to worship him. – Raymond C. Ortlund

Several years ago, newspapers told how a new Navy jet fighter shot itself down. Flying at supersonic speed, it ran into cannon shells it had fired only a few seconds before. The jet was traveling too fast! You are also traveling too fast, if you don't have time to worship God in regular church services, if you don't have time to read the Bible, if you don't have time to pray. If you're neglecting any of these, you're probably traveling too fast to hear the sound of God's voice. You can't tell whether you are in the center of His will. Better slow down before, like the jet, you shoot yourself down.

Epilogue

Dear friend, no one can fully comprehend all you have seen, witnessed, and experienced. Even those who were part of the same tragic event will learn to live with it differently because of the way they processed the event.

People are the only unique beings that can deny, accept, reject, minimize, exaggerate, avoid, play down, refuse, give up, admit, recognize, acknowledge, and endure such events. The core to successfully processing all the non-sensory and sensory information your mind and emotions were bombarded with is linked to knowing Christ Jesus. Knowing Christ is the crucial key to be able to accept, understand what you witnessed, and see this event in a different light than most would.

Christ wants you to come to Him to find answers He knows you are ready to receive. He invites you to come to Him for rest, not to shun Him because you might believe He is unloving or impotent to stop the free will of wicked men.

This Bible says,

> "Come now, and let us reason together," (Isaiah 1:18a)

> "Come to Me, all who are weary and heavy-laden, and I will give you rest. (Matthew 11:28)

I truly pray and hope that you have begun to recognize that God deeply loves you and desires you to be well and enjoy living life, and living life to the fullest through these studies. Perhaps there are issues I failed to include. If that is the case, please feel free to contact me with your questions and I promise I will respond to you with the best biblical insights I know. You can e-mail me at mcmbclsor@yahoo.com.

If you want to speak to a biblical counselor in your area, go online at www.nanc.org. Click on NANC Counselors. A drop down box appears. Click on Certified Counselors List. You can search by "zip code."

There may be continuing counseling resources at our web site: www.mtcarmelmin.org. Printed and audio resources are available on a variety of topics at affordable prices. You can also view and read current and past newsletters on an assortment of topics.

About the Author

Dr. Richard Thomas, D. Min is the Founder and Executive Director of Mt. Carmel Ministries. He is married and has four adult children. Rick is a graduate of Moody Bible Institute, Chicago, IL. and earned his Masters of Ministry, masters of Divinity, and Doctorate in Ministry from Trinity Theological Seminary, Newburgh, IN.

Rick has served as a pastor, educator, conference speaker, and counselor. As an author, Rick has written several books, including Restoring Truth to Counseling: Foundation for Change, Worship: A Life in Turn with God, Masturbation: Shattered Expectations for Sexual Gratification, and King David: God's Man with Feet of Clay

Rick has developed counseling-training curriculum and counseling aids in a variety of media formats. Rick publishes a free monthly newsletter called Today's BIBLICAL COUNSELOR. He is a Fellow with the National Association of Nouthetic Counselors and member of the International Association of Biblical Counselors.

MCM maintains a web site (www.mtcarmelmin.org) and blog site (www.mtcarmelmin.org/blog). You can contact Dr. Thomas via e-mail at mcmbclsor@yahoo.com.

2879254